Bible Unlocked

Revealing new meanings
from the original Greek

Kristina Kaine

DEDICATION

I dedicate this book to you, my reader. May you discover your True Self nestled within your soul.

"Difficult, unpleasant hours come to every esoteric striver, and then it's good to have some support. We find this support in the New Testament; we find advice and support for every case and situation and in every weakness; we only have to look for it. And if we don't find it, we can comfort ourselves with the conviction that it's our own weakness that keeps us from finding the right thing but that it's nevertheless in the Bible." Rudolf Steiner
From the Contents of Esoteric Classes 24 August, 1910

CONTENTS

ACKNOWLEDGMENTS

I acknowledge all my loyal readers over many years who express their appreciation for my work.

Words like this inspire me.

"I am a lifelong Christian; but not a bible study kind of person -- because I never really understood it. I have been reading your writings on Revelations and find it understandable and inspiring."

FOREWORD

The Bible is not a "religious" book; it is a sacred book of mysteries hiding the secrets of civilization from misrepresentation and even corruption. This book can help you unlock the Bible to make your own discoveries.

These words from Rudolf Steiner explain why I write about the Bible, trying to nut out the inner meaning - or as I put it, the esoteric meaning - that lies just beneath the surface of the words.

"The New Testament stands as a record for humanity — but the whole future course of the Earth's evolution will be required to reach a full understanding of the New Testament. In the future, men will acquire much knowledge of the external world and of the spiritual world also; and if taken in the right sense it will all contribute to an understanding of the New Testament.

The understanding comes about gradually, but the New Testament is written in a simple form so that it can be absorbed and, later, gradually understood. To permeate ourselves with the truth that resides in the New Testament is not without significance, even if we cannot yet understand the truth in its deepest inwardness. Later on, truth becomes cognitional force, but it is already life-force, in so far as it is imbibed in a more or less childlike form." Christ and the Human Soul: Lecture 4 Rudolf Steiner

Over the years many people have emailed feedback about my writing, their words make me very humble while at the same time inspiring me.

I wanted to let you know that your words DO inspire and encourage me -- to think new thoughts and reach new understandings. Thank you so much for sharing. Your words are a blessing.

I have been enjoying these insights for some time now; but today I have a

new awareness of the absorption of these ideas into my psyche. Before, these insights were 'interesting'. Today they are 'informing'; meaning that I sense them as creating in me a new attitude and positionality in the world and within myself. This change carries with it greater confidence and strength and intentionality, and consideration of the spiritual beings in the surround.

Thank you greatly for your writing, the interpretation of the Bible into personal development has been of enormous encouragement for me in everyday life .... thankyou, thankyou........ it has given me great purpose in living and many great hints in handling daily experience.

1 INTRODUCTION

Sacred texts are intriguing and although they can be difficult to read, we often find little gems that shine like diamonds in our minds. It is as if they have the power of a seed to sprout over time, tickling the brain with a new thought. We can find inspiration in any of these ancient books; The Bhagavad Gita, The Vedas, The Tanach, The Quran or The Bible.

Previously it would have been necessary to be a devotee of a particular faith before we were given access to its sacred texts. Not only that, only a few hundred years ago many people could not read, but also, only the religious leaders were allowed to read these sacred texts to their followers according to certain guidelines.

Today, many sacred texts are freely available on the internet and especially on The Sacred Text Archive www.sacred-texts.com/hin/index.htm

The Purpose of the Bible

When I began these articles, my intention was to put forward various ways to open up the Bible so that it can make more sense to our modern minds. I hoped to appeal to anyone regardless of their religious beliefs as well as those with no religious beliefs.

Many theologians and church leaders, who influence vast followers of organized religion, have a very limited view of what the words in the Bible mean. Some even go so far as to suppress its meaning so that they are in a position of control over their congregations; one example among many is Papal Decrees.

Then, even those who have glimpsed inner meanings in the Bible apply them in a narrow way. Instinctually – perhaps influenced by past life memories –when some people are presented with Biblical stories they enter into a mystical feeling element of religiosity at the expense of clear thinking. It is almost as if people get drunk on scripture and cannot see or hear into the true meaning of the words. We could call this blind belief although those who experience it would strongly disagree. For them it is a real experience but they cannot express it clearly in words indicating that it does not enter their ability to think, therefore they have no ideas about their experience.

Still others, who are able to think about what they read don't like what they see and are unwilling to measure their own activity by what they read. Then, the other way is to reject scripture and religion – perhaps because it is seen to be nonsense; what they hear expressed by those who say that they know makes no rational sense.

This is a major problem to be faced in the immediate future as we are forced to make sense of this world and our place in it. Rudolf Steiner spoke the words below in 1912 which shed some light on our task. May I add that many of his adherents have no interest in the Bible or what he had to say about the entrance of Christ into the man Jesus. I suggest that this is exactly the issue the church faces – picking out the bits they want to understand, the bits that suit their purpose, and discarding the rest. I speak plainly here without the intention of damaging anyone's ego – each of us is called to examine how our ego responds to anything that we read and if we can engage our I Am and become the interested observer we will see elements of truth in my words.

It remains to be said that the deed of Christ was for all humanity, the various religious beliefs are different ways to experience this deed. If we can open our hearts and appreciate how each person experiences the presence of Christ – even if they don't call it that – in whatever religion or philosophy they dedicate themselves to, we are standing in the purpose of the deed of Christ which at its core says, "Love one another." *Muslim*

These are Rudolf Steiner's significant words spoken almost 100 years ago. As we read them we can ask ourselves how we have contributed to the founding of this universal Christianity.

"Indeed, it has often been emphasized that in [evolutionary] developments such as those here referred to, all that has taken place since the Mystery of Golgotha is not particularly meaningful. As yet everything is only at the beginning; only during the future evolution of the earth will the great impulses that may be ascribed to Christianity make themselves felt. Over and over again we must emphasize the fact that Christianity is only at the beginning of its great development.

If we wish to play a part in this great development, we must enter with understanding into the ever increasing progress of the revelations and impulses which originated with the founding of Christianity. Above all we are required to learn something in the immediate future; for it does not take much clairvoyance to see clearly that if we wish for something definite to enable us to make a good beginning in the direction of an advanced and progressive understanding of Christianity, we must learn to read the Bible in quite a new way.

There are at present many hindrances in the way, partly because of the fact that in wide circles biblical study is still carried on in a sugary and sentimental manner. The Bible is not made use of as a book of knowledge, but as a book of common use for all kinds of personal situations. If anyone has need of it for his own personal encouragement, he will bury himself in one or the other chapter of the Bible and allow it to work on him. This seldom results in anything more than a personal relationship to the Bible.

On the other hand, the scholarship of the last decades, indeed that of virtually the whole nineteenth century, increased the difficulty of really understanding the Bible by tearing it apart, declaring that the New Testament is composed of all kinds of different things that were later combined, and that the Old Testament also was composed of many different parts which must have been brought together at different times. According to this view, the Bible is made up of mere fragments which may easily produce the impression of an aggregate, presumably stitched together in the course of time. This kind of scholarship has become popular; very many people, for example, hold that the Old Testament is combined out of many single parts. This opinion disturbs the serious reading of the Bible that must come in the near future.

When such a serious way of reading the Bible is adopted, all that is to be said about its secrets from the anthroposophical viewpoint will be much better understood." Rudolf Steiner, St Mark Lecture September 16, 1912

The question then arises about how we might understand Bible texts. This has been my mission for well over thirty years. Beginning on New Year's Day in 2003 I began writing about hidden meanings in the Bible. These hidden meanings are not associated with any religious philosophies; they apply across the board and appeal to many kinds of readers. I have published many books containing what I have written during this time.

I would like to take you on a journey through the Bible, mostly the New Testament, to show how it has carried the secret to human evolution safely into the present. I will start by explaining how some of the words translated into English lose their true meaning. I will also explore ideas about the makeup of the human being as body, soul, spirit, and 'I' which are necessary if we are to make full sense of what the Bible actually means. On this journey we can discover the evolution of human consciousness and see how it plays out in our own minds.

As I use many quote from the work of Rudolf Steiner, this summary of the core of Rudolf Steiner's teachings may be helpful:

1. Humanity has evolved as a result of the dialectics between forces and counter forces in the spiritual worlds.

2. Earthly lives are repeated in a variety of spiritual ways, the valuable components are preserved for later use.

3. Evolutionary forces changed human consciousness, new soul qualities are developed at certain intervals.

4. The mystery of Golgotha is the centrepiece of evolution, but the influence of the Christ impulse was manifest long before the birth of Jesus – see Buddha, Zarathustra, Moses.

By Peter Mollenhauer, from the Introduction to "The Principle of Spiritual Economy" by Rudolf Steiner

2 THE THREEFOLD HUMAN BEING

Body, Soul and Spirit

One of the great difficulties of revealing the inner meaning of Bible texts is the lack of understanding about the makeup of the human being. We are not just physical bodies; we have a soul and spirit and the Bible recognizes this.

Let's explore the three elements of human beings as they are found throughout the Bible. Take this text for instance.

"May the God of peace himself sanctify you wholly; and may your spirit (pneuma) and soul (psuche) and body (soma) be kept sound and blameless at the coming of our Lord Jesus Christ." 1 Thessalonians 5:23

Why would Paul bother describing human beings in this way? Never mind what he meant by "be kept sound and blameless at the coming of our Lord Jesus Christ." I will come to that because it doesn't mean what we think it does.

One of the first hurdles to overcome when reading the Bible is our understanding of the nature of the human being which is usually limited to its physical substance of flesh and blood. When we look closely at human nature we can easily understand how the expressions of body, soul, and spirit are quite different from each other.

Furthermore, if we think about ourselves and how we function in the world, we know we are beings who think ideas; who have sensations - feelings, and emotions; and who act according to how we think and feel. Awareness of these three essential human faculties; feeling, thinking and acting (will), are also necessary to make sense of human nature. They are tangible; we experience them every moment of each day. Furthermore, each of these three faculties has a specific connection to our body, soul, and spirit, as we will see.

Referring back to the text quoted above, *psuche,* from which we have the word psychology, is translated in the Bible as heart, life, mind or soul, and refers primarily to our soul which gives us our capacity to feel and sense things. *Pneuma* is translated as breath, life, spirit, or wind, and describes our spiritual nature which is associated with our ability to think - it is suggestive of thoughts that can blow through our mind. Our body, which is the earthly vehicle of the soul and spirit, in the Koine Greek is *soma,* the center of human activity and mobility, which we can identify with human will.

We can apply these ideas to the following text from 2 Corinthians,

"For we know that if the earthly tent [physical body] we live in is destroyed, we have a building from God [spiritual body], a house not made with hands, eternal in the heavens. Here indeed we groan, and long to put on our heavenly dwelling, so that by putting it on we may not be found naked. For while we are still in this tent, we sigh with anxiety; not that we would be unclothed, but that we would be further clothed." 2 Corinthians 5:1-4

This shows us how these bodies are referred to in other

ways. It is interesting to note that it is without our spiritual body that we are naked. This is a direct reference to events in the Garden of Eden when Adam and Eve saw that they were naked. They divested themselves of their spiritual body to take on a physical body.

Now let's look at the words from Thessalonians 1 5:23, *"kept sound and blameless at the coming of our Lord Jesus Christ."* They have a very specific meaning, which in broad terms refers to the work we must do to become aware of our full human potential. The word 'sound' is *tereo* which means to watch, observe, to become conscious of. What are we to become conscious of? Ourselves as beings of body, soul, and spirit.

Blameless is *amemptos,* which means perfect, without fault and is a direct reference to our values and motives. Are our actions motivated to benefit ourselves, or for the benefit of everyone, including ourselves? This text is really recommending that we become conscious with good values and motives. It is surprising to notice how we change when we consider these small things about ourselves.

Armed with these few simple principles we can step into the Bible and discover new meanings.

Exploring Feeling, Thinking and Will

When interpreting the Bible, as we have seen, it is important to know that Esoteric Christianity recognizes the threefold human being of body, soul and spirit and it is also important to align them with the three basic human faculties of will, feeling and thinking (in that order).

We have our physical body in common with the mineral kingdom. Our physical body has life because of the presence of a life-force which is called the etheric body. This force is associated with the human drive to survive; to eat, to regulate temperature and comfort, to regenerate and procreate. Humans have this in common with the plant world. Think of an apple; on the tree it is plump, when left in the fruit bowl it gradually shrivels and rots. This happens because its etheric life-force depletes. If our etheric body disconnects from our physical body we die. There are several Greek words in the Bible that mean life and refer to our etheric body; *bios, psuche* and *zoe*. In this way we can say that *bios* is physical life; *psuche* is soul life; and *zoe* is spiritual life.

Our physical body has movement and experiences emotion because of our astral body or desire body. We have this in common with animals. For instance, plants cannot move around as animals do because they do not have this astral body. We can also call this astral part of us our soul body. If our astral body disconnects from our etheric and physical bodies we become unconscious and unable to move. In the Bible, the words *soma* and *sarx* refer to our astral body. The various words for desire point to the lower or higher motives of the astral body; *thelo* – to wish, *epipotheo* - to lust, *epithumia* – to crave or covet, *eudokia* – good pleasure.

The evolving human being refines their astral body through becoming conscious of exactly how they feel, think, and will. The activity of these three human functions is actually our soul. The more conscious these functions are the more active is our soul. When the word *psuche* is used in the Bible it points to the activity of the soul.

When we achieve a certain level of consciousness in our feeling, thinking, and will, and only when we do, can we become aware of the human 'I'.

Becoming aware of the self in its lowest and highest expressions is, in fact, our life's purpose. When we are not aware of this 'I' component in our being it works in us as a reflection, as a mirrored image. In its lower expression, it is egotistical and selfish. This is a necessary part of our development because it makes us aware that we are individuals responsible for our own welfare. Once we experience this selfishness, we must immediately raise it up to a higher expression. Then we experience ourselves as independent, self-aware, individuals. The highest expression of the human 'I' is referred to in the Bible as *ego eimi*. The ability to say 'I Am' is to have full self-consciousness.

As we become aware of the activity of the 'I', then the third part of our being, our spirit, comes to life. This is referred to as *pneuma*. The three activities of our spirit are Imagination, Inspiration, and Intuition. We have experiences of these functions when we are able to raise our feeling, thinking and willing to a higher expression through a conscious connection with our 'I'.

When reading the Bible it is helpful to see which of these Greek words is used. It is surprising how often they are mistranslated, and when we assign the right part of the human being to the text, the meaning can change significantly.

Discovering the Real Human Being

To unlock anything we need tools, unlocking the Bible requires specific tools. The most important tool, as we have been considering, is to have a clear understanding of who we are as human beings. This could be why the image of a physical man nailed to a cross, who then goes through a resurrection, is burned into our consciousness. The truth about human nature has been blurred for centuries, by the church and by science. For this reason many texts in the Bible don't make sense, especially when we compare them with the fundamental meaning of the Hebrew or Greek words.

As we begin to understand the makeup of a human being we can also begin to know ourselves more deeply. There are many ways to approach this but let's begin with our physical body. How strongly do we identify with our physical body, thinking that this is who we are?

Then we hear mention of the soul. Where is this soul and what does it do? We also hear a confused mix of references to our soul and our spirit. The way these terms are used can lead us to believe that they are interchangeable. Certainly the translators of the Bible confuse these terms.

As mentioned above, the Greek terms are body *soma;* soul *psuche;* and spirit *pneuma.* Searching for these terms in the Greek interlinear Bible can be surprising because we see how a text can have a different meaning if these words are translated accurately.

It doesn't take a lot to understand the difference between our body, our soul, and our spirit. In my book "I Connecting" I write in detail about the difference between these three areas of our being, and many who read it and study it have come to know and understand themselves in a way that assists them to take greater charge of their lives.

Let's look again at the human being as a being of body, soul, and spirit. Then we can discover how each of these three aspects has three functional parts. We can put it simply in this way:

1. The body is physical, it grows, and it moves.

2. The soul feels, it thinks, and it has intentions (will).

3. Through the spirit we develop higher faculties of Imagination, Inspiration, and Intuition.

The I Am

All of these elements within us are governed by what the Bible refers to as the I Am. We can call this I Am the Higher Self. It is the highest expression of what we experience when we say "I". The way the I Am or Higher Self interacts with us is mostly unconscious and it is our job to develop a conscious awareness of it.

We hear about this I Am in the second book of the Bible when Moses has his famous conversation with God. Moses asks God what his name is (Exodus 3:14) and the response is *Ehyeh asher ehyeh* which means I Am that I Am. In the New

Testament we meet the I Am in the Greek expression *ego eimi.*

The ancient Greek Philosopher Philo wrote of this event which speaks of the I Am and of God.

"There was a bush or briar, a very thorny plant, and very weak and supple. This bush was on a sudden set in a blaze without any one applying any fire to it, and being entirely enveloped from the root to the topmost branch by the abundant flame, as though it had proceeded from some fountain showering fire over it, it nevertheless remained whole without being consumed, like some impassible essence, and not as if it were itself the natural fuel for fire, but rather as if it were taking the fire for its own fuel." Philo

The most important purpose we have on this earth is to become aware of our I Am. We could say that this I Am expresses itself in us as two egos. Much of the information about them is confusing. Calling the second ego an "Ego" causes great confusion. The second ego is the Higher Self, the I Am.

We experience both egos when we say "I". As Rudolf Steiner says in his first lecture on the Gospel of St John, 24th June, 1909 *"for 'I' must be spoken within us: to everyone else we are 'you'."* This in itself shows us that our ego-being is distinct from all else that is in or around us. Then he says, *"within this ego another, a higher one, is born, as the child is born of the mother."*

We might ask if this second ego replaces the first ego. This is not the case; our task is to manage them both. As Steiner explains, *"a second 'I' that can say "you" to the first one in the same way that the 'I' itself says "you" to the outer world and to its own body — that looks upon this first 'I' from above, as it were."*

This means that we must learn to be aware of which ego is working within us at any given time. One place to start might be to have a conversation with ourselves from the perspective of each ego. If, for instance, we become angry, can we pause long enough to establish which ego is angry - are we having an reactive outburst of anger, or is it so-called 'righteous anger' rising up within us.

Distinguishing between these two egos is ongoing, and any assistance we can get will be helpful. Steiner continues to explain. *"[The second ego] is linked with the imperishable, just as the first ego is bound up with the perishable, the temporal; and by means of rebirth this higher ego can behold a spiritual world just as the lower ego does perceive the physical world through eyes and ears."*

As we work with our two egos, we reach a point where we experience the presence of Christ - in this world and in us. *"This means that just as a rebirth can occur for the individual in his development, so a rebirth for all humanity came about through Christ Jesus."*

Steiner continues,

"And what is it that is reborn? When a man observes his inner self, he finally comes to realize that what he sees there is that to which he says "I". Its very name differentiates it from anything in the outer world. To everything in the outer world, a name can be applied externally. Everyone can call a table a table or a clock a clock; but never in the world could the name "I" fall on our ear if it were intended to denote our self, for "I" must be spoken within us: to everyone else we are "you." This in itself shows us that our ego-being is distinct from all else that is in or around us.

But in addition, we now come to something that spiritual scientists of all times have emphasized from their own experience for the benefit of mankind: that within this ego another, a higher one, is born, as the child is born of the mother. A man as he appears in life is first encountered as a child, awkward in his surroundings but gradually learning to understand things: he gains in sense, his intellect and his will grow, and his strength and energy increase. But there have always been people who grow in other ways as well, who attain to a stage of development beyond the average, who find, so to say, a second I that can say "you" to the first one in the same way that the I itself says "you" to the outer world and to its own body — that looks upon this first I from above, as it were.

As an ideal, then, for the soul of man, and as a reality for those who follow the instructions of spiritual science, we have the thought: the ego I have hitherto known takes part in the whole outer world, and together with this it is perishable; but there slumbers within me a second ego of which men are unaware but can become aware. It is linked with the imperishable, just as the first ego is bound up with the perishable, the temporal; and by means of rebirth this higher ego can behold a spiritual world just as the lower ego does perceive the physical world through eyes and ears.

This awakening, rebirth, initiation, as it is called, is the greatest event for the human soul — a view shared by those who called themselves confessors of the Rose Cross. These knew that this event of the rebirth of the higher ego, which can look from above on the lower ego as man looks on outer forms, must have some connection with the event of Christ Jesus. This means that just as a rebirth can occur for the individual in his development, so a rebirth for all humanity came about through Christ Jesus. That which is an inner event for the individual — a mystical-spiritual event, as it is called, something he can experience as the birth of his higher ego — corresponds to what occurred in the outer world, in history, for all mankind in the event of Palestine through Christ Jesus." Rudolf Steiner The Gospel of St John Access this lecture online at www.rsarchive.org

Distinguishing Between Soul and Spirit

Let us now continue to explore in more detail the soul and the spirit. Only when we look at these aspects of the human being from many different angles will we begin to identify them in our own lives.

Thomas Moore, the American psychotherapist and author, had some great things to say about the difference between the human soul and the human spirit in an interview with Oprah (google it). He spoke about the movement of the spirit and the attachment of the soul. This is a great way of distinguishing the difference between our experience of soul and spirit. Why do we need to differentiate between soul and spirit? First and foremost, it gives us more awareness and more control of our responses to life.

Attachment, while giving security, can also be painful. Movement gives the experience of freedom. When I am aware of my inner attachment and movement then I can work out how to move from being attached to feeling free. Although, the feeling of attachment, as Thomas says, gives us a sense of where we belong, of our family, friends, and colleagues, yet at the same time, we must admit that strong attachment can bring pain.

Not that pain is a bad thing, it certainly has its place in making us stronger, but being aware of the patterns of attachment and freedom means that we are more self-aware. I know that if I become too attached to an idea that doesn't work, or a person I have outgrown, I have to go through a stressful separation. I have experienced relief from this stress through the movement of my spirit. This usually arises when I see the possibility of a new idea, a new friend, or a new opportunity.

As discussed above, by exploring the ancient Greek language used to write the New Testament we can discover the importance of identifying the specific words for spirit — *pneuma*; soul — *psuche*; and body — *soma* or *bios*. In the Bible these three words can be mistranslated or confused. We are so aware of our body, and the way it is in touch with the outside world, there is a tendency to think that we are only physical beings. The translation of sacred texts comes into question when the word body is used instead of soul or spirit. The translators may not have been aware of the difference it makes to speak of the soul or the spirit.

This takes on more meaning if we consider that our spirit and soul use our body, bios, our biology, as a means of expression. Compare this to a motor vehicle: The driver is the spirit, the engine equates to the soul, both working through the body of the vehicle. We know that a vehicle isn't of much use without an engine and a driver.

Awareness of Soul and Spirit in daily life

This leaves us asking how we can be more aware of our soul and spirit. The best place to start is to think about how we connect to the outside world. The outside world enters into us through our senses. All that we see, hear, and feel enters into our soul and there we make sense of what is outside us. If the sensory impulse is familiar, we are quickly able to identify it, but if we see or hear something for the first time, it can take a while to figure out what it is.

A good illustration of this is a story about Charles Darwin's voyage to South America. They anchored the ship, the Beagle, and went ashore. It was a large ship, larger than the natives had ever experienced before. A sailor asked a native what he thought of his ship, and the native replied through the interpreter, "What ship? All I see is a large bird out on the water."

I often think about this story to help me become aware of the activity of my soul; I see something, then I think about it, giving it personal meaning, and then I can act on what I saw, or decide not to do anything. This is what happens in my soul. As Thomas Moore says, we do this with attachment. We all have certain feelings and thoughts about things, and we have particular patterns of behavior. This comes up in our relationships with our friends and family. We hear people say, "Oh, dad won't like that." Or, "What will mum think of that?" "My husband/wife/friend won't be happy when I tell them about that."

If we can overcome our initial reaction to situations, detaching from our habitual responses, then the movement of our spirit assists us to be more accepting of another person's behavior. The movement of our spirit opens us to the future. The spirit moves in our soul, making it more mobile and pliable. Through our spirit, we can change, releasing ourselves from past patterns that hold us back. Those who allow this movement of the spirit within their soul are usually more content with life, more inspiring, accepting change and changing themselves to meet the future.

3 THE WORD

The Word of God

The Bible is often referred to as the Word of God. This word is said to be powerful but do we really understand the power of the word? Nikola Tesla, the inventor, made this interesting observation.

"Every one should consider his body as a priceless gift from one whom he loves above all, as a marvelous work of art, of indescribable beauty and mastery beyond human conception, and so delicate and frail that a word, a breath, a look, nay, a thought, may injure it."

Do we really have the freedom to say what we like or even think what we like? How often do we stop to consider the impact of our words on another person before we speak? If we are angry with them then probably rarely do we think of how our words affect them. Yet, we only have to think about our own response to the way some people speak to us to realize the truth of Nikola Tesla's words.

Harsh words, words spoken in anger, insults, create wounds in the soul. We could even say that if we let an insult fester in us, we intensify the wound.

The Nature of Logos

Examining the true meaning of the word 'word' will give us greater understanding of Nikola Tesla's ideas. The *Word*, in New Testament Greek, is *Logos* and it is an important word in the Bible. It is so important that John uses it to begin his Gospel, *"In the beginning was the word"*. To the Apostle John the *Word* or *Logos* means much more than a simple word; in the *Logos* word and concept become one. This means that if we experience the *Logos*, we live in the concept the word describes, and we experience a full understanding of it. This is an 'aha' moment. Unfortunately today the world is drowning in words that are mostly misunderstood.

When John speaks of the *Word,* the *Logos,* he means a spoken word that creates something.

When does a spoken word create something today? Perhaps we can call it creative when it inspires, for example, during a motivational talk, or at school when the words used by a teacher ignite the life path of a student. Although, as Nikola Tesla says, the word can also be destructive.

With these ideas in mind we can look at the words used to begin the Gospel of St John. They are not usually translated accurately. The following is a more considered translation.

In the beginning was the Word (Logos), and the Word was with God, and the Word was a God. The same was in the beginning with God; all things entered into existence through it and without it nothing entered into existence. In it was life, and the life was the light of mankind. John 1:1-4

The Word-seed

So if this *Word*, this *Logos*, was a God, what exactly was it? We can gather some helpful ideas from Mark as he reports on the parable of sowing the seed. After he told the parable of sowing the seed on rocky ground, among thorns, or on good ground, he said privately to his disciples that the *"sower sows the word (logos)."* Mark 4:14

This parable explains that the word is a seed and the way that it is planted matters. While the word remains a seed it is mute, the seed only speaks when it becomes the plant it is destined to become and bears the flowers and fruit it is intended to bear.

This also tells us of a creative process, a birth process. When we speak we give birth to words, we conceive them, then we form them, and then we let them go.

It follows that when we become aware of this primal *Logos* resonating through us, we are in touch with the creative impulse of the Universe. We could also say that this word is a universal form of communication, a universal language we must awaken within us. We know that words are what connect us to each other, when one speaks and the other hears we are joined by the *Word*, the *Logos*. When the Word is expressed in its purity, out of love, we experience grace.

As John tells us, from the very earliest beginnings the *Word*, the *Logos*, filled Cosmic space with the sound of creation. If we think of sound as a note, we know that a note must have a perfect tone otherwise it is discordant. If we can hear the original sound, we know that through it we can make sense of the mysteries that underpin human life. This is our challenge, to get in touch with the *Creative Word*, the *Logos* - that which was in the beginning.

The Birth of the Word

In 2005 I wrote a more detailed explanation of the Prologue of the Gospel of St John which is worth considering now before we move on to exploring the mystery of Jesus and Christ.

"In the beginning was the Word, and the Word was with God, and

the Word was God. He was in the beginning with God; all things were made through him, and without him was not anything made that was made. In him was life, and the life was the light of men. There was a man sent from God, whose name was John. He came for testimony, to bear witness to the light, that all might believe through him. He was not the light, but came to bear witness to the light. The light shines in the darkness, and the darkness has not overcome it. There was a man sent from God, whose name was John. He came for testimony, to bear witness to the light, that all might believe through him. He was not the light, but came to bear witness to the light. The true light that enlightens every man was coming into the world. He was in the world, and the world was made through him, yet the world knew him not. He came to his own home, and his own people received him not. But to all who received him, who believed in his name, he gave power to become children of God; who were born, not of blood nor of the will of the flesh nor of the will of man, but of God. And the Word became flesh and dwelt among us, full of grace and truth; we have beheld his glory, glory as of the only Son from the Father." John 1:1-14 RSV

The Logos

This is the wonderful, powerful prologue to the Gospel of St John that we are told the Essenes chanted to assist the incarnation of Christ.

The Word or *Logos* cannot really be understood by minds that only take in what the eyes physically see and the hands physically touch. We can only start to understand the Logos with a thinking that is active, always striving to see new connections. These connections are not so obvious; they lie beneath the surface seen only by those taking a second glance.

Today we are unaware of how significant this Logos is in life as we know it. John tells us that the Logos is the beginning and the end of the story, the alpha and omega, the first as well as the last. We exist because of the Logos – *"all things were made through him"* - and we have life and light through this Logos, and we will experience our own resurrection through this Logos. These explanations often leave us struggling to have images in our minds. Yet without these images our modern consciousness cannot fathom this strange, esoteric language.

So what is this mysterious Word, this Logos that we hardly understand yet it made us? It isn't God because John points out that *"the Word was __with__ God."* Even though the text then says *"and the Word was God"* - the translator left out a tiny word, it should be *"and the Word was 'a' God."* So there was more than one god; 'he', the Logos, *"was in the beginning with God; all things were made through him, and without him was not anything made that was made"*. Does this mean that the Logos was some sort of instrument, or even a companion of God in the beginning when all things were made?

We may find a clue in Genesis where something similar but different is written:

"In the beginning God created the heavens and the earth. The earth was without form and void, and darkness was upon the face of the deep; and the Spirit of God was moving over the face of the waters. And God said, "Let there be light"; and there was light." Genesis 1:1-3

Speech

It is always good to take the Bible literally, particularly when the Greek translation is applied to the meaning. If we take the word 'Word' to mean the words we use in our thinking, our speech and our writing, instead of the lofty, unfathomable, Cosmic principle 'Logos', we may be able to make more sense of the introduction to the Gospel of St John. We may also be able to see the connection with Genesis.

Look at it from this approach. What actually happens when we speak? Couldn't we say that when we speak we give birth to words? First we conceive them, then after a period of gestation we expel them out of the womb of our throat. Doesn't this make the ability to speak a sacred thing? Doesn't it point to the power that exists in speech which therefore makes speech a God-like action?

So what about the connection between the two texts? In Genesis God 'said', God spoke everything into being. On the other hand, in the New Testament, John points out that in the beginning it was God and the Word (the Logos) together making all things, bringing things into existence.

In Genesis the first thing that God spoke was, "Let there be light." In John's Gospel it says, "*In him was life, the life was the light of men. The light shines in the darkness, and the darkness has not overcome* (comprehended) *it.*" Later on in his Gospel, in chapter eight, John records that Jesus said, "*I am (ego eimi) the light.*" Doesn't that mean that the I Am is the light? Here the mystery is resolved. The I Am was there in the beginning. Genesis doesn't speak of the I Am as directly as John because it wasn't until the birth of Christ Jesus that the gift of the I Am was given to individual human beings. John is heralding this new advent, this new beginning, when he says God and the Logos / Word were a creative team who worked with the I Am, the light.

Therefore during the Advent Festival is an excellent time to reflect on the Prologue. If we recite the Prologue each day through December it will change the way we experience the birth of Christ Jesus through the Advent-Christmas-Epiphany period.

In this way we have the opportunity to experience the power that builds up within our being which can give us a different understanding of how we give birth to words. Through the Advent period we could also try to make a point of observing how we use the power of speech. What do we actually give birth to when we speak? What do we create? Are our words *"full of grace and truth"*?

Grace

When our words are full of *"grace and truth"* we behold the glory of Christ, the radiant presence of Christ. This presence doesn't just stand there shining, it teaches us, and it fills us with knowing. All too often the word grace, *charis*, is said to mean getting something for nothing, or being given something that we haven't really earned. *Charis* is not about taking; it is about giving, and giving powerfully. When we give power through our speech, when we are at one with those we speak to, this power is a shared experience between equals. There is no thought of what might be received, but only what is given. As soon as we think of what might be received, the power is gone. When this power is shared, teaching takes place. This is not about one teaching the other it is about a shared knowingness. That is the true meaning of grace, *charis*. For this reason grace is a sacrament.

Of course, we know that what is given must be received but always the focus must be on the giving. Some say that since Golgotha we automatically receive the gift and the giver. If this is true and no effort is required on our part, why aren't we all perfect now! While we can accept that Christ continually gives of his substance, surely it is only when we become conscious of the giver and the giving that it truly becomes a gift. The Christian church has been quite misleading about this. Be good boys and girls, come to church on Sunday, swallow what the minister puts on the spoon, gulp it down, no need to chew it - understand it - and you will go to heaven. Nothing could be further from the truth. It is only when we are conscious of the Word becoming flesh, that is, dwelling in us, that we receive the grace, the power, and the knowing, not before.

Grace, *charis,* is also a deed of love. It is created out of nothing, out of the beginning. Too often we love because something happens to make us love; this love is born out of something. In other words, we love when the conditions are right.

When love arises out of nowhere, for no apparent reason,

it creates something very powerful. We experience this love without jealousy, envy, or guilt, without any feeling of possession. The power of grace gives us the experience of pure love. This love is voluntary and is expressed by those who are becoming conscious of their eternal being, of their Logos being.

Communication

In his book "Becoming Aware of the Logos", Georg Kühlewind, the Anthroposophical philosopher, says *"Love is the word's wing – without it, the word cannot fly"*. So this mighty Cosmic Word is actually our communication with one another. What is the quality of our communication? Do we give enough attention to what we say and how that affects those who hear what we say? Furthermore, if the Word is our communication doesn't this mean that our communication is a sacred act?

We experience this when we yearn for the ability to say the right thing at the right time. It takes a lot of effort to search for the right words that will express a thing sacredly. When the ideas expressed by the words ring true we are lifted up and a light shines in the darkness.

When words are used to manipulate others a darkening occurs and the sacred is excluded. When important conversations are not had, when people avoid communicating with each other, the sacred is excluded. On the other hand, today, mountains of words are spoken, like formulas; clever, persuasive, seemingly insightful, yet empty. In fact, they kill the sacred Word.

The Word and the I Am

The sacred Word can only be spoken by those who have a strong connection with their I Am. There is much confusion about the I Am, let's just recap so that we are all on the same page. Our I Am is outside us, like the mother-ship. The small 'I' that we express when we say "I am hungry or cold" is not the I Am, it is the mirror image of the I Am - for when we look in the mirror the image we see is not us, it only resembles us.

On the other hand, Christ is in us. He shed his blood into the earth and it is the earth that provides the substance for our physical body. Everything we eat builds up our body and fills it with Christ. Not many people are conscious of this. As we become more and more conscious of the presence of Christ within us (and around us), then Christ has to be 'crucified' in our physical body so our small 'I' is resurrected in our etheric body where Christ will quicken our connection with our I Am. So while we strengthen the connection with our I Am, and Christ becomes more active in our being, then there is less of the mirrored reflection and more of the 'reflected one' working in our life.

When we contemplate the Prologue and the Word, it is through the I Am, our Real Self that we have the ability to speak. Only human beings can speak, only human beings can think about what they will say. Any so-called speech or thinking from the animal kingdom is mere mimicry or instinct. Think about the importance of the first words a child utters. We could say that it is an Advent-time in every parent's life when they eagerly wait to hear their child's first words. These are sacred words and they herald the coming of the I Am into the flesh. When the child masters a certain number of words they begin to think, again it is the presence of the I Am that facilitates this thinking. Another Advent-time for parents is when they see their child's first steps. Our ability to stand upright is only possible through the influence of the I Am.

Language

The uniqueness of human beings is that they use words to communicate with each other. As Georg Kühlewind points out, the essence of this communication between us is the Logos. It can be helpful to think of the Logos as a spiritual being; the governor or guardian of language. It is almost strange to contemplate that while words remained unspoken different languages do not exist. Regardless of our race or culture the thought of a house, a dog or a man is the same. Thanks to the events of the Tower of Babel human beings began to individualize through the word. This individualization takes place in the soul and produces different soul moods according to our geographic location. In our I Am, however, we experience the unity of the human race. This is a work in progress, for now we can observe how this individualization develops in modern culture.

It is taken to the extreme when people speak in jargon - a pretentious or meaningless language that excludes others. True individuality does not exclude others; it includes them with full respect for their individual expression. Today's jargon turns Babel into Babylon, which the Book of Revelation refers to as a harlot.

"on her forehead was written a name of mystery: 'Babylon the great, mother of harlots and of earth's abominations.'" Revelation 17:5

The pure essence of the Logos is prostituted by jargon because no images can rise up in our soul out these barren words, words which should be connecting human beings together regardless of race.

The Effect of Words

It is important to realize that the words we speak don't just have an effect on the being of the person who hears them; they have a profound impact on our own being. The more we are aware of this the more careful we are with our speech, and the more economical we are with our words. This is why my spiritual mentor, Rev Mario Schoenmaker, so often asked us not to talk so much and encouraged us to sit in silence together more often.

There is a little exercise we can do to experience the effect of what we say. In a quiet moment sit still and say to yourself, or to a friend, the words, "I am". Say it over a few times and then observe how you feel as these words echo through your being. Then say the words, "I am not". Notice the difference between the effects of these two statements.

If we don't experience the sacredness and preciousness of words we do not have any hope of connecting up with our I Am. Our experience will be 'I am not'. This also means that we cannot experience the present. Only when we say, "I am" can we experience the present. The 'I am not', negates the present, it refuses to stand in the present. 'I am not' is busy reliving the past or it can't wait for tomorrow. 'I am not' avoids the present, avoids the I Am - of self and of others. Meanwhile, the sacred Word, which is always spoken in the present, doesn't have a place in our lives.

The Self-born

Finally John says:

"And the Word became flesh and dwelt among us, full of grace and truth; we have beheld his glory, glory as of the only Son from the Father."

This last verse of the Prologue is so powerful and so full of meaning. Georg Kühlewind reveals something very interesting about the words *"only Son from the Father"* which makes perfect sense when we apply them to our understanding of the I Am.

In the Greek these last words of the Prologue literally say this:

And the Word flesh became and tabernacled among us, and we beheld the glory of him, glory as of an only begotten from a father, full of grace and of truth.

That phrase 'only begotten' is *monogenes* which literally translates as 'one-born' … or self-born! That is the secret of the I Am, it must be self-born. No one can connect us with our I Am but ourselves. We must do the work. We must not reject our I Am. Through knowledge, through inner teaching, we behold the glory; we shine with the radiance of the I Am that we have given birth to in our own soul.

The concept of being self-born is very important if we are to understand human purpose. We find it also in Luke's gospel:

On the next day, when they had come down from the mountain, a great crowd met him. And behold, a man from the crowd cried, "Teacher, I beg you to look upon my son, for he is my only child; and behold, a spirit seizes him, and he suddenly cries out; it convulses him till he foams, and shatters him, and will hardly leave him. And I begged your disciples to cast it out, but they could not." Jesus answered, "O faithless and perverse generation, how long am I to be with you and bear with you? Bring your son here." While he was coming, the demon tore him and convulsed him. But Jesus rebuked the unclean spirit, and healed the boy, and gave him back to his father. And all were astonished at the majesty of God. Luke 9:37-43

These words, *"And behold, a man from the crowd cried, "Teacher, I beg you to look upon my son, for he is my only child"* reveal a mighty secret. *Epiblepo epi ho huios ego hoti monogenes ego eimi* means, 'perceive my offspring; the self-born, *monogenes*, of my I Am'. This man has given birth to his own I Am through his own effort. He is now presenting himself to his teacher Jesus who has given birth to his own I Am before him.

Furthermore, when we do this work, then the spiritual worlds fully understand the importance of the Logos becoming flesh as described by John. We forget that the beings in the spiritual world can only experience this earth through us. Advent is that time of the year when the Angels draw close to the earth. They will draw closest to those who have the radiance of the self-born. Because the Angels can see all the beings of the Cosmos co-operating with each other to create the rhythm of the Cosmos, we can share in this. Therefore, Advent gives us the splendid opportunity of not only experiencing the Angels and their view of the heavenly

Cosmic beings, but also we can be conscious participants in this work. The aim is so that we experience the birth of Christ consciously within our own souls which in turn is experienced in the Cosmos. Contemplating the Prologue enhances this.

As Paul says in his Letter to the Romans: *"For the creation waits with eager longing for the revealing of the sons of God;"* Romans 8:19

In the light of all this we can consider a slightly different version of the St John's Prologue which takes into account most of the ideas we have contemplated here. These words are combined from my own understanding of the translations of Rudolf Steiner, Rev Mario Schoenmaker, and Georg Kühlewind. We can never be prescriptive about translating this mysterious chant. Hopefully we will continually find new meaning within the words. This is just one version; there are many others.

Those who are trained in Eurhythmy, where each word is spoken with reverence and clarity so that the essence and spiritual truth of the word is expressed, could try speaking this prologue and possibly it will induce powerful rhythmic images in your minds. Whenever it is spoken with deep reverence it can give a sense of how this Essene chant assisted the incarnation of Christ.

In the beginning was the Word, and the Word was with God, and the Word was a God. The same was in the beginning with God; all things entered into existence through it, and without it nothing entered into existence. In it was life, and the life was the I AM of men.

The I AM shines in the darkness, and the darkness has not comprehended it. There was a man sent from God, whose name was John. He came as a witness to the I AM, that all might believe through him. He was not the I AM, but was a witness to the I AM.

It was the true I AM that illuminates the complete-human (fully human) *that is coming into the world. The I AM was in the world, and the world came into being through the I AM, yet the world did not know the I AM. The I AM entered into individual beings, and the individual beings received it not. But to all those who received the I AM, to those who believed in the name I AM, the I AM gave power (exousiai) to become children of God; who were born, not of blood nor of the will of the flesh, nor of the soul's will, but of Spirit. And the Word became flesh and dwelt within us, teaching us, as the radiance of the self-born Son of the Father, full of grace and truth.* Adaptation by Kristina Kaine

4 JESUS AND CHRIST

Who is Jesus Christ?

As we have been discovering, understanding the true meaning of words in the Bible unlocks the meaning of this ancient and sacred text. Before we go any further, we need to look at the central character in the New Testament, who is often referred to as Jesus Christ. Is this one being or two different beings?

A survey of the New Testament reveals that we rarely find the names Jesus and Christ expressed together. This is an important observation because not only are they two different beings, they are not interchangeable. We can only understand this if we understand who these beings are. To begin with, one is a human being; the other is a spiritual being.

In the Gospel of John for instance the name Jesus is always used alone except in two places:

1:17 *"grace and truth came through Jesus Christ," and,*

17:3 *"And this is eternal life, that they know thee the only true God, and Jesus Christ whom thou hast sent."*

In fact, Paul reverses the names to Christ Jesus. This could suggest that Christ is a title; like saying Queen Elizabeth.

If we read the New Testament with this in mind, a new story unfolds. Here is a man called Jesus, *Iesous,* meaning savior, who becomes Christ, *Christos,* meaning anointed, or we could say Jesus becomes Christ-ened. This is our task too, but it is not plain sailing as Matthew points out in his discussion of the *pseudochristos* or false Christ:

"For false Christs and false prophets will arise and show great signs and wonders, so as to lead astray." Matthew 24:24

Evolving Consciousness

If we take the Bible as a manual for evolving human consciousness then we could have a goal to become like Jesus striving to achieve Christ-ened perfection. The New Testament is full of descriptions of the nature of Jesus and how this nature might be attained, or followed. The word follow is *akoloutheo* that literally means 'alike-way' and gives the sense of becoming like Jesus, copying the way he is. The way he is has been greatly misunderstood.

When considering human consciousness it isn't enough to say human beings are conscious and have consciousness. This state of being awake and aware clearly differs from person to person and changes within each of us throughout the day. Nor is it sufficient to say things like; I am health conscious, I have a national consciousness of shared beliefs and feelings, or I lose consciousness if I faint, or the way I think represents the kind of consciousness that I have. This is generalizing, skimming the surface of what it means to be conscious.

To fully understand consciousness means to consider it in detail. Human consciousness has three core activities: feeling, thinking, and willing. We each use these activities differently, and in different combinations.

These three activities actually take place in the human soul, *psuche*. We form our feelings, thoughts, and actions in our soul and express them in our body. The more aware of this we are, the more conscious we are.

In the biblical Greek there are more than thirty different words for these three activities. If we look up "An Expository Dictionary of New Testament Words" by W.E. Vine we find fifteen words for think, five for feel and seven or more for act, commit, do (will). Each particular word reveals a specific quality of human consciousness, and a particular aspect of our soul, and it is in the specific use of these words that the real wisdom of the Bible unfolds.

Aristotle (384BC-322BC) was among the first to write about the human soul. Prior to this, it wasn't necessary to write anything about the soul because the soul wasn't differentiated into different activities as it is today - pointing to the fact that human consciousness changes.

Aristotle was aware that a differentiation was taking place which led him to describe the soul as having three qualities that he called: Orektikon, Kinetikon, and Dianoetikon.

1.   Orektikon refers to desires, appetites, sensations, impulses which is the soul activity of feeling.

2.   Kinetikon means to set in motion, to try every way, reasoning, which is the soul activity of thinking.

3.   Dianoetikon is about intention that is the soul activity of will.

By taking these things into account, the difference between Christ and Jesus, representing the evolution of consciousness, makes a lot of sense. Jesus had to prepare himself by becoming more aware of his consciousness, giving him the ability to be as objective as possible when he was treated the way he was.

Understanding this, we can follow Jesus on his journey to Golgotha and see how the human being makes way for the spiritual being to arise. Jesus was able to bear all things through his ability to be fully aware of his feeling, thinking, and will, just as we are able to bear life's difficulties when we control our feeling, think clearly, and act consciously.

When Jesus Met Christ

Let's now look more deeply into the details about Jesus and Christ being two different entities. They do become one eventually, in full maturity, in a similar way to a child growing in the womb, being born, and developing into an adult over time.

What is the point of understanding the process of Jesus taking into himself the Christ we may ask? Isn't it simpler and easier to worship the one being and to be done with it? In fact, why even differentiate between God, the Father, Christ, the son, and the Holy Spirit?

If the detail is not important, why does the Bible have so much detail? Surely not so that we can boil it all down into a few basic ideas! What would be the point of that?

We unlock the Bible when we look into the detail and see its place in human evolution, and in our own lives - that is its point and purpose. The Gospels tell us quite clearly that Jesus began his intimate relationship on this earth with Christ at his Baptism when he was 30 years of age. For this reason, the Gospels of Mark and John begin with the baptism of Jesus. Matthew and Luke begin with the birth of Jesus and that is a story for another time.

It is also interesting to note that Jesus is not referred to as the "Son of God" until after the baptism.

A thorough study of all four Gospels shows that each writer looks from a different angle at the life of Jesus; the first time their views coincide is with their accounts of the baptism.

"Prepare the way of the Lord, make his paths straight." Matthew 3:3, see also Mk 1:2-3, Lk 3:4-6, Jn 1:23

The Role of the Holy Spirit

The baptism of Jesus is celebrated each year on the sixth of January with the religious festival of Epiphany. The word *epiphany* is a combination of two words, *epi*, meaning on, to, and *phainein*, meaning to show. Epiphany then means to manifest, to come into view, to be on show. At the baptism of Jesus, facilitated by John the Baptist, the physical appearance of the mighty Cosmic Christ Spirit manifested. How did it manifest? Like a dove. Let's look into that.

In those days Jesus came from Nazareth of Galilee and was baptized by John in the Jordan. And when he came up out of the water, immediately he saw the heavens opened and the Spirit descending upon him like a dove; and a voice came from heaven, "Thou art my beloved Son; with thee I am well pleased." Mark 1:9-10

We find three main points in the accounts of the baptism; heaven opened, spirit descended as a dove, and the Son of God is announced. The dove is the sign of the Holy Spirit, always the precursor to the Son, as the Son is the precursor to the Father. John explains:

"These things I have spoken to you, while I am still with you. But the Counselor, the Holy Spirit, whom the Father will send in my name, he will teach you all things, and bring to your remembrance all that I have said to you. John 14:25-26

If Christ was already present in Jesus why send the dove / Holy Spirit? We can look at these beings as The Trinity, or we can look at them individually to see the different work done by each one. We can also ask, if Jesus and Christ were one being all along, was this baptism necessary? Also, why was it suggested that John the Baptist might be the Christ? Read what Luke says.

As the people were in expectation, and all men questioned in their hearts concerning John, whether perhaps he were the Christ, John answered them all, "I baptize you with water; but he who is mightier than I is coming, the thong of whose sandals I am not worthy to untie; he will baptize you with the Holy Spirit and with fire. His winnowing fork is in his hand, to clear his threshing floor, and to gather the wheat into his granary, but the chaff he will burn with unquenchable fire." Luke 3:15-17

Jesus was no stranger to these people; he was part of their life, working as a carpenter. If Jesus and Christ were one, why would people say John might be Christ? Luke also says they *"were in expectation"* which means they knew something was going on, just as we sense something is going on in our own lives at times.

What was going on here was the entrance of the mighty Christ being into the earth, or at least the beginning of the process. It was begun by the Holy Spirit. Jesus was the most pure person on the whole earth able to withstand the power of these heavenly beings. Taking the Christ into himself took three and half years. It wasn't until he was nailed to the cross, immobilized physically, that the Christ could enter fully into him, right into his bones - which is why *"Not a bone of him shall be broken."* John 19:36

Understanding these details can give us a greater sense of expectation during the Easter Holy Week if we walk to the cross with Jesus knowing him more completely.

It Took Two Jesus' to Make THE Jesus.

It is no accident that the genealogies in St Matthew and St Luke's Gospel are different. One traces the ancestry of a highly developed human being living on this earth. The other traces the spiritual legacy of a pure human spirit incarnating for the first time on the earth. What we see here is wisdom in one and innocence in the other.

The question we can ask is this. Could Christ, a mighty

Cosmic Being beyond our understanding, who had never experienced life in a physical body on this earth, just be born through a mother as we all are? That would be like saying the sun could enter this earth and shine from within it.

By looking closely at the two genealogies, it is not difficult to see that two different Jesus children were born to two different Marys, with two different fathers called Joseph. The Matthew Jesus descends from the Solomon line of the House of David. The Luke Jesus descends from the Nathan line of the House of David. If we look into our own genealogy, we know that we are quite different from our cousins whose parents were siblings of our great grandparents - if we multiply that for all the generations mentioned in the Matthew and Luke Gospels we get the picture.

The Matthew Jesus child was the product of 42 preceding generations from Abraham to Joseph. Kings visited him when he was born, whereas shepherds visited the Luke child. The Luke Jesus' genealogy reaches back to Adam when human beings first left their spiritual domain and took on flesh - as told in the story in the Garden of Eden. These details are very important yet often skipped over.

I have written about this in detail in my book "Who is Jesus : What is Christ?" Vol 1. Why mainstream theologians do not explore this information is a mystery. Others have written about it and some artists have painted the two Jesus children. In his painting, Madonna Del Duca di Terranuova, Raphael has painted the two Jesus' with John the Baptist and the Luke Jesus' mother.

Not only that but also these children were born at different times. The Matthew Jesus was older, born at the time when Herod ordered all male children to be killed.

"One notable fact is that Herod ordered all male children aged two and under to be killed, which led to the Matthew Jesus being taken to Egypt, there is no mention of the child described by Luke going to Egypt. Even John the Baptist, who Luke tells us is 6 months older than the

Luke Jesus, seems to have escaped Herod's horrendous order, supporting the fact that these children were born at different times and in different places." Who is Jesus : What is Christ? Vol 1 by Kristina Kaine

To make sense of this story we also need to keep in mind that Jesus and Christ are different beings. Matthew states it clearly when we read the original Greek. Immediately after the genealogy he writes: *"Now the birth of Jesus Christ took place in this way."* In the original Greek it says, *tou de iesou christou he gennesis outos ne* which more accurately translates as 'of the **yet anointed** Jesus the origin thus was'. Christ comes from christos, a Greek word meaning 'anointed.' Matthew is saying Jesus is yet [to be] anointed, Christen-ed, which points to the future baptism.

In the Temple

Before that can happen, these two Jesus children will become one. We read about this event in Luke when Jesus' parents lost track of him. They found him three days later and he was a changed person.

After three days they found him in the temple, sitting among the teachers, listening to them and asking them questions; and all who heard him were amazed at his understanding and his answers. Luke 2:46

If we put ourselves in Joseph and Mary's shoes as they entered the temple and found their unearthly, innocent son - autistic in today's terms - in deep dialogue with the teachers in the temple, we can experience their amazement. These teachers had devoted their whole lives to understanding the sacred texts and here was a twelve year old boy matching their understanding! What was incredible to the parents, was perhaps understandable to the teachers who knew what was about to take place when they found the two Jesus boys together in the temple. The painting called, "The twelve-year-old Jesus in the Temple" by Borgognone, a fresco in San Ambrosius in Milan, shows the true nature of this event. For this reason, this image is on the cover of all volumes of "Who is Jesus : What is Christ?"

In this fresco, the Luke Jesus sits on the throne having just assumed the wisdom of the Matthew Jesus, who then leaves the temple. In the painting, all eyes are on him as recognition of his mighty sacrifice. Now the innocent Jesus takes on earthly wisdom. This is part of what it takes to prepare for the entrance of the Christ into this earth. This twelve year old boy will grow into a thirty year old man and meet his childhood friend John the Baptist by the river Jordan where the Holy Spirit, which always precedes the Christ, can enter into him.

Two Jesus boys + Jesus & Christ = I Am, Our True Self

The Bible remains locked to us if we gloss over the facts. Examining the difference between Jesus and Christ while exploring the purpose behind the birth of two Jesus children, as well as the baptism of Jesus, does not completely make sense unless we understand the reason why Jesus was born in the first place. He didn't come to save us; he came to show us how to save ourselves!

To express it in the simplest way possible: a human being was required - Jesus - to take into himself a mighty Cosmic being called Christ, so that every human being could personally experience the I Am.

What is this I Am? The first time we hear about the I Am is after Moses sees the burning bush which is not consumed, and then he has his famous conversation with God. Moses asks God what his name is, and the response is *Ehyeh asher ehyeh* I AM that I AM (Exodus 3:14). As previously mentioned, we also find this term I Am in the New Testament in the Greek words *ego eimi*.

Before the time of Christ, human consciousness was not sufficiently developed to experience the I Am. To have this experience required high levels of initiation as was the case for the great initiate Zarathustra. The only way the general population could experience the I Am was in a secondhand way through Elijah in the Old Testament, and Krishna in the Bhagavad Gita.

Only through the birth of two Jesus boys, as well as the baptism of the 30 year old Jesus when the Christ Spirit entered into him, could we have this personal, firsthand experience of the I Am. Because of Zarathustra's initiation into the experience of the I Am before its time, he played an influential role in this process through his involvement in the birth of the Matthew Jesus. A second Jesus, described by Luke, whose pure being was not tainted by life on this earth, was also required.

Why did this I Am take so many convoluted paths before it became accessible to human beings? The short answer is that it can't just be given to us we have to earn it. Human consciousness had to evolve to a point where it could handle the power of the I Am, and it has been a long time in the making; from Adam to Elijah to Jesus and now to us. The power of the I Am is like fire; it must burn in us but not consume us as the story of the burning bush reveals. One way we can recognize it in our consciousness is when we are angry but the anger does not consume us.

What is the I Am?

Is this I Am God or is it human? Well, simply put, it is both. The I Am is that part of God that is in us. Its main role is to make us creative, as God is creative. Whenever we express our talent, in those amazing moments when we do great things, it is the I Am expressing itself in us. We also see it when people who don't like each other ignore their differences and work together, for example, in an emergency. The I Am knows no boundaries of creed, gender, color, or nation.

A powerful example of the nature of the I Am arose in a

conversation between the British interviewer, Michael Parkinson and Paul McCartney which went like this:

"This is just me in here. Paul McCartney is some guy over there doing amazing things. If I thought that was me constantly it would blow my head off."

The I Am is certainly a mysterious and powerful element of the human being. It can make us anxious and even fearful. Perhaps for this reason, knowledge of it has been hidden from us by the churches and secret societies down the ages. The time has come for us to be aware of it and to use it to the best possible effect in our lives. The challenge is that we have to discover it ourselves; it can't be taught. We can read about it but then it is up to us to have our own firsthand experience of it.

Every detail in the Bible about the life of Jesus shows us how we prepare ourselves to work with the I Am. The ideas later on in this book about Repent, Sin, and the Word, introduce us to ways in which we can strive to become fully human, which means fully integrated with our I Am. In my book "I Connecting" I explain it in a non-religious, psychological way.

While I recommend the Bible to discover the true meaning of the I Am, I must stress that it is not about any specific religion; each religious expression is a path up the mountain to the pinnacle of knowledge of the I Am. Nor is it about dogma and definition, this knowledge must become alive in us as we strive to become aware of our own true nature, that is, to really know ourselves.

I am always uplifted and inspired when I read the final words in St Matthew's gospel: "I am with you always, to the close of the age." In the Greek it says: *ego eimi*, I Am, always with you till the consummation of this period of time.

Contemplating the *ego eimi* statements in the Bible is one good way to awaken to the activity of the I Am within us.

The I Am is the musician who plays the instrument of the soul.

Becoming a Christ

The Bible is the story of the developing human spirit. The books of the Bible tell us where we came from, where we are going, and how to get there. From the very first words in Genesis, to the very last words in The Revelation, the story of the human journey, in the presence of Christ's activity, is revealed.

The ultimate goal is to become Christen-ed. I use this word purposefully because the being we call Christ is the human archetype. We strive to be like him. John speaks of this.

"Beloved, we are God's children now; it does not yet appear what we shall be, but we know that when he appears we shall be **like him**, for we shall see him as he is." 1 John 3:2

In other words, we become a Christ. Paul speaks about this often, particularly in this statement:

"I have been crucified with Christ; it is no longer I who live, but Christ who lives in me; and the life I now live in the flesh I live by faith in the Son of God, who loved me and gave himself for me." Galatians 2:20

"Not I but Christ in me" is one of the highest goals in our spiritual development. Some people think that it is beyond our reach in this lifetime, others are put off by the religious connotations. Both these responses reveal a misunderstanding of the true nature of these words.

If we examine the Greek words in Galatians 2 closely, a new picture emerges. Let's take the words one by one. Christ, *Christos* meaning anointed, to crucify *sustauroō*, with a stake, the flesh to live *zao*, spiritual living, no longer I *ego* but in my *Christos,* my anointing, and in the present time live, *zao,* spiritual life, in my flesh *sarx*, astral, to live *zao*, with faith *pistis*, which means a conviction based on hearing, and the son of God that loves, *agapao*, the highest love, and gave, *paradidōmi*, which means giving in close proximity himself for my sake.

One way to paraphrase this would be to say that Christ pins the astral body and our ego down and gives it spiritual life. This is an ongoing process. At present, as our astral body is being given spiritual life, we are anointed and we can hear the inner word from the loving son of God who gives himself to us for our sake.

To fully understand what this is saying it is helpful to remove from our minds any religious ideas and images that we might have. They often hamper us from grasping these important truths. St Paul is telling us about the activity of Christ within our being. It pins down our astral, anoints it, which raises it from physical life to spiritual life, so that we hear the spiritual love of the son of God, which comes to us as Inspiration - we inspire words of truth and they echo inside us. This is why Christ came so that he could continually pour from himself all that is necessary for us to become him, to be anointed as he is.

So how does this play out in our lives? Let's say that someone annoys us. Their behavior irritates us and our animosity intensifies. This activity takes place in our astral body. Our emotions become agitated. As we experience this happening, we can bring to mind this idea of Christ pinning down our astral, quietening our emotions. Then we can think to ourselves; Not I but Christ in me. Then we can say, "If 'I' can't love them then let me experience how 'the Christ in me' can love them. Then the anointing takes place within us. We become Christ-ened and our lower responses are resurrected.

Therefore, Christ is the model for what we are to become. This mighty Cosmic Being who had never experienced this earth before, entered into the human being called Jesus, to show us what is possible. John puts it this way:

"Truly, truly, I say to you, whoever believes in me will also do the works that I do; and greater works than these will he do, because I go to the Father." John 14:12

What is Christ?

To understand what this means in our lives, we must first try to understand what Christ is for us. This is not about being religious, nor is it about attending a particular church. Christ is a spiritual force present in the whole of humanity; this force is present in every human being, in nature, in this earth and in the Universe.

In his highest expression we can call him the Cosmic Christ and find him as part of the Trinity; Father, Son and Holy Spirit. At the other end of the scale we can see him in the body of Jesus who lived on this earth. This spectrum from mighty spiritual being to human being is the story of the Son of God becoming the Son of man. His journey is revealed in the Bible as well as in the many myths and legends passed down through the ages.

The immediate question arising from this is why. Why would such a mighty being bother to come to earth? Surely not to save us from our sins - wouldn't that be a bit trivial? Since sin, *harmartia*, means 'missing the mark' nothing should interfere with us perfecting our aim. Why would we let someone or something else shoot our arrow for us?

One simple reason this mighty Christ Spirit made the journey into the sphere of this earth was to save this earth, to give it a new lease of life, thus enabling us to improve our aim. His union with the body and blood of Jesus, and the subsequent gushing of blood from Jesus' side when he was struck with a spear, enabled the spirit of Christ to literally penetrate this earth and hence **every** human being on this earth who eats food grown in the earth.

This is the basis for the Last Supper when Jesus explained

that the bread, a product of the earth, was his body, and the wine made from sun-ripened grapes was his blood. While this event is celebrated during Holy Communion, we can also celebrate it every time we eat. As we take food into our mouths we can think of the journey Christ made through the spiritual spheres of the Universe to enter into us; first into Jesus beginning with the Baptism, and then through the crucifixion entering into the earth where our food is grown.

Why Did Christ Come to Earth?

The reason he came to the earth is directly connected to a new phase in the development of the human being. He didn't come to take something away from us (sin), he came to give us something which we could not access by ourselves - our Higher Self, our True Self, which is our I Am.

We should not take this idea of Christ entering into a human body too lightly. It was not an easy thing to achieve. If we read the accounts of the crucifixion from the point of view of Christ's difficulty rather than Jesus' difficulty, we can come to new and different understandings. What was it like for a mighty being who had no idea what it was like to live in an earthly physical body, whose consciousness had no limits, to be confined in Jesus' body? We could liken it to a university professor suddenly having to use the mind of child.

Let me recap in very simple terms what I have come to understand and experience about this event over many decades. Jesus was the most highly developed human being ever born, his purity exemplified by his mother, the Virgin Mary. His journey to the cross was a series of events that prepared him to fully receive into himself the Cosmic Christ. Jesus was a vessel prepared for generations through the Hebrews so that he could be the channel for the Son of God to enter into a human body. In so doing, he showed us how to follow in his footsteps and prepare ourselves to become aware of our True Self and awaken the presence of Christ within us.

Our immediate response might be to say. "I want that." Yet, we have to be able to bear the powerful presence of Christ. Since Golgotha, Christ is within us as a potential, as a seed, to which we must give life. As we know, no seed can survive without being nurtured.

In the esoteric lesson of 27 May 1909 Rudolf Steiner says in this regard: *The true name of Christ is "I am"; who does not know or does not understand this and calls Him by another name does not know anything about Him. "I am" is His only name.'* GA 266/1. See also the lecture of 9 January 1912 in GA 130.

Purpose of Christ

I received this message which echoes many people's experience of Christ. "I get a bit lost, or put off, when Steiner makes the "Christ event" so central to his thesis (also true to a degree with your writings)."

To understand the Christ event is quite a challenge. It comes with so much baggage; we are either attracted to, or repelled by, this Being for our own personal reasons. Furthermore, these reasons could stem from experiences in past lives, a notion which increasingly makes sense to me.

So should the Christ event have a central place in our lives? If so, why? Let me put the case for the centrality of Christ.

Evil Has its Place

The forces of evil are so misunderstood today. Why are we so keen to be rid of them when they could be of great assistance when seen in the right light.

In my series "Who is Jesus : What is Christ? I wrote this.

'We could also ask: Is the Son of man glorified because Judas goes out, or because Judas received the morsel, or because of what left Jesus and entered into Judas?

We might be able to answer this if we consider how we achieve the status of the Son of man, huios ho anthropon. It is reached when we free our thinking, feeling and will from our body so that they function spiritually, no longer needing physical stimuli – in other words, we give birth to our highest human potential. Would we need to free ourselves of Satan to achieve this status? If this is what happened, then Judas has given a great service to Jesus by carrying away any remaining anti-force that was within Jesus." Vol 5

It strikes me as highly credible that Judas, one of the intimate group of 12 disciples, put his hand up to carry out this essential task so that in total purity Jesus could fully receive into himself the spirit of Christ making the crucifixion and resurrection possible.

Understanding the Human I-being

If we understand that human beings are at a higher level than animals, plants, and minerals (while containing these principles within them), what is it that sets us apart? Essentially it is our ability to truly stand upright, to speak words, and to think (especially complex and logical ideas). We have this ability through what Steiner (and many others) terms our I-being. When we say "I" we can only mean ourselves.

One of the reasons that we do not understand this I-being is because we cannot identify its properties within us or around us. We do begin to understand it in our love for ourselves. Our love for ourselves, however, is fraught with difficulty and the industry of psychology has arisen around this. If we can experience this love for ourselves we then become aware of the individual that we are. There is however a point where this self-love can be overdone. Self-love is simply part of the process.

In order to move to the next level where we could experience this I-being in a self-less way we needed the missing ingredient. We need to have a personal experience of the Higher Self, the higher I-being or the I Am. This I Am experience is the pinnacle of human experience. As previously mentioned, we were introduced to it in the story of Moses and the burning bush when (a) god said that his name was I Am.

Purpose of Love

From this story we come to know that this I Am has the properties of fire – not just any fire but a fire that does not consume. Take a leap here and think about this fire as love. We certainly know about the concept of consuming love. So is there another kind of love which we are yet to experience? Is this why Jesus spoke of a new Commandment; love one another? (Read more about this in the essay on The New Commandment.)

We know that throughout human history right up until the present time we have had pioneers who show the way: they have an experience first and then they share it with others. The leap humanity experienced from self-love to selfless love needed a pioneer and that pioneer was Christ. Christ, through the Holy Spirit, brought the fire (at Pentecost) into individual human beings. No other being could have done this. And no-one will experience it unless they prepare themselves. This fire is the I Am and if we were to experience it unprepared we would get severely scorched.

Not only did Christ have to bring this experience into individual human beings, he had to bring it into the earth itself. The constitution of the earth was completely changed when the Cosmic Christ entered step by step into the man Jesus, into his blood, which then flowed from the cross into the mineral condition of the earth. No other being in the entire Universe, not even the Father, could have accomplished this. In this way the Christ event is central and pivotal to the human experience and to human evolution. We carry it in our ability to love one another.

When we Think of Christ do we Think of his Team?

If the crucifixion of Jesus is to become more meaningful for us at Easter we can turn our attention to the many spiritual beings that made the crucifixion possible. Jesus did not act alone, and Christ, who had never experienced an incarnation on this earth before, certainly could not have acted alone. It is also worth noting that Christ had never experienced death before.

We have two beings going through an incredible transformation. Jesus is absorbing the mighty Cosmic Christ and that took its toll on his physical body; and Christ is losing his Cosmic identity as he works out how to occupy this physical body specially prepared for him.

It is a birth and a death rolled into one; Christ is born in Jesus and at the same time dies to the spiritual worlds. This exchange of power also had an enormous impact in the spiritual worlds because they felt the consequences of the departure of Christ as they had known him.

The main beings who worked directly with Jesus and Christ to make the crucifixion possible are the Nathan Soul, that pure human element that incarnated for the first time on earth into the Luke Jesus. The Master Jesus, the highly developed soul incarnated into the Matthew Jesus who donated his body to the 12 year old Nathan Jesus in the temple. Vidar, Buddha's guardian angel, who thereby earned a promotion to Archangel, but elected to stay back to assist with the Christen-ing of Jesus. Finally, the Archangel Michael, who had earned the status of Archai, but like Vidar, knew he had a greater role to fulfil with the incarnation of Christ.

The purpose of this Easter event is so that every human being can experience Christ in their souls. We will do this with more success if we think about these beings who still work for the full realization of Christ on earth. They do it in this way.

o   The Nathan Soul leads to a more intimate sense of the constant Christ presence within the human soul.

- ○ Vidar reveals the path of beholding Christ in etheric form through the development of new clairvoyant faculties.

- ○ Michael reveals Christ as Lord of Karma and assists us to bring our individual karma into equilibrium in such a way that this process can best serve the further evolution of all mankind.

- ○ Master Jesus, in his connection with the great initiate Zarathustra, is the inspirer of those who strive to understand Christianity, especially the great event in Palestine, in its living growth and development.

If we hold these beings in our hearts, especially when we seek a more immediate experience of the Christ event, they will reveal to us what we are ready to see.

Ideas taken from The Cycle of the Year as a Path of Initiation by Sergei Prokofieff.

What is Blood?

Many religious festivals are overlooked today. We are happy to have holidays for Christmas and Easter even if we have no connection to the reason for the holiday. In many ways an overly zealous church has alienated us from them. However, we do not need to be affiliated with a church to bring the meaning of these festivals into our lives. They belong to the whole of humanity because they are connected with the development of human consciousness. They are also connected with the birth of Christ Jesus who entered this earth for all of us.

Not only did he live on this earth but his blood flowed out of his body and into the earth itself. We could say that it soaked the earth with the purity of its forces. If we eat food grown in this earth then surely these forces enter into us, consciously or unconsciously. If we are to understand the consequences of this act we need an understanding of what blood actually is. In his play Faust, Goethe wrote, "Blood is a very special fluid." Rudolf Steiner explains this in his lecture given in October 25, 1906 www.rsarchive.org

Steiner explains that essentially blood is our liquid life; it is like a second being in us, distinct from our bone, muscle, and nerve. The latter connects us to this earth and our blood connects us with the higher worlds and with our Higher Self, our I-being. The purpose of the crucifixion and the resurrection was to assist us to purify ourselves so that we could become aware of the spiritual worlds through our connection with our Higher Self. With this in mind consider these words in the Gospel of St John.

So Jesus said to them, *"Truly, truly, I say to you, unless you eat the flesh of the Son of man and drink his blood, you have no life in you;* John 6:53

If we examine the meaning of some of these words the symbolism referred to by the Church moves beyond the symbol and becomes a reality in our own being. There are nine different words for eat in the Greek. Each one has a specific meaning. The word *phagō* is used here and it means to consume or devour so that whatever we eat unites with us inwardly and becomes part of us.

The flesh of the Son of Man does not refer to the physical body of Jesus. The word for flesh here is *sarx* which means our astral body. The astral body gives us consciousness and is the seat of our desires which we need to purify. The Son of Man is that state that we attain as we are able to carry out this purification. We, Man, give birth to the Son. We regenerate our desires, refining them and raising them ever higher. See the ideas about being self-born previously discussed.

Pinō, to drink, is to receive into the soul what will nourish it. The blood, *aima*, of the Son of Man is our own blood which we have individualized and purified so that we can become aware of our I-being which our blood carries. The highest expression of this I-being is the I am and Christ is the archetype of the I AM.

If we can do this we will have life in us. Life, *zoe*, is our spiritual life. Remember, as previously considered, that the other words for life are *bios* which is physical life, and *psuche* which is soul life.

What St John is saying in this text is that in every moment of our life we can participate in the process of consecrating our own being. We do this by responding to life in the highest way possible. We become one with our purified astral body which means that our consciousness is heightened, and we individualize our blood, we claim it away from our ancestors and make it our own. In these ways our Higher Self influences our feeling, thinking, and will; our three basic soul forces. That is what blood is for, to give us our true spiritual life here on this earth so that we can know the truth of our own existence. Without blood we could not be consciously aware of whom we really are. That is the real mystery of blood.

What is Sacrifice?

As we think of the mission of Jesus we should turn our attention to his mightiest deed - the Sacrifice. What are we to make of the sacrifice of Christ Jesus as we stand in the twenty-first century? Sacrifice is not a popular concept today. It is either rejected completely as we look after 'number one', or it is taken up wholeheartedly in the sacrifice of self for others. Both are examples of the egotism that drives the modern human being.

When we contemplate the Easter Festival, the image of sacrifice can be overwhelming. A physical body hanging from a cross with nails hammered through hands and feet, is a horrendous thing to contemplate. Our instinct is to look at it from a distance. John, in his gospel, tells us that this was the popular choice. Only one of Christ Jesus' disciples, accompanied by the three holy women, could stand beneath the cross to which he was nailed, and look closely at what had occurred.

But standing by the cross of Jesus were his mother, and his mother's sister, Mary the wife of Clopas, and Mary Mag'dalene. When Jesus saw his mother, and the disciple whom he loved standing near, he said to his mother, "Woman, behold, your son!" John 19:25-16

In his lectures, Rudolf Steiner repeatedly advised us to make the event of Golgotha a living reality in our soul. The interpretation of this event over the last two thousand years has hardly given us any tools. In fact, many of the ideas etched within our being from childhood contribute to the Mystery of Golgotha remaining a mystery. Now it is for us to crawl out from under the many ideas that bury the deed and see its true purpose.

A good place to start is to explore our understanding of what a sacrifice actually is. Our modern understanding of the nature of sacrifice is that we deprive ourselves of something so that someone else benefits. We might, rightly, look to the motives behind such actions.

Is this really what sacrifice means? If we look to the Latin roots of the word: *sacer* "sacred," + root of facere "to do, perform," then sacrifice is a sacred action. Through our actions, we can make something holy. Therefore a sacred action usually points to a consecration or a transubstantiation; changing something physical into something spiritual; something lower into something higher. This is quite different from the notion of depriving ourselves so that others may benefit; this idea of sacrifice suggests that everyone benefits. Furthermore, doesn't this idea of sacrifice lie behind our motives to develop spiritually? True spiritual development means that the effort of each person benefits the whole community.

The Bhagavad Gita and the Bible Meet

In the Bhagavad Gita there is a wonderful story which speaks about this idea of sacrifice. In his lectures, published as The Bhagavad Gita and the Epistles of St Paul, Rudolf

Steiner spoke about this. It is a story about what happens when we leave the heavens and enter into earthly life. From the heavens, we look down on our planned biography and see the many conflicts we will encounter with those who incarnate with us through our karmic relationships. In the Bhagavad Gita Krishna advised Arjuna in this way:

"if you can rise above all this [conflict] and not be affected by your own deeds, like a flame which burns quietly in a place protected from the wind, undisturbed by anything external: if your soul, as little disturbed by its own deeds, lives quietly beside them, then does it become wise; then does it free itself from its deeds, and does not inquire what success attends them."

Steiner goes on to explain that whenever we perform a deed, *"there is something which at the same time is a looker-on at these deeds, which has no part in them, which says: I do this work, but I might just as well say: I let it happen."*

Being able to live quietly beside all that happens in our lives is the sacrifice. We sacrifice our self-absorption in our own problems and live quietly beside the problem while it reveals its purpose to our quiet observation.

This is the experience of connecting with our I Am. Even though the full expression of our I Am is a work in progress, we can still experience something of this eternal human being within us now – if we work towards it, if we sacrifice. In the Bhagavad Gita, Krishna is our I Am and Arjuna is its mirrored reflection - that part of us that incarnates to work towards an ever-higher consciousness.

Sacrificing the Lower Self

This would suggest that sacrifice is the purification of our lower self. Therefore, we have the opportunity in all moments of our daily life to sacrifice. Each time our natural instincts and our habitual behavior influence the way we think, feel, and act, we have the opportunity of sacrificing or making holy these soul faculties. For instance, if we meet someone we dislike, we have the opportunity to find something likeable about him or her. This means sacrificing our instinctive dislike – often originating from a past-life memory.

Or it could be something that we do, for example, drawing or painting. We may feel defeated at the thought of drawing a picture, but if we can sacrifice the feeling of defeat, we free ourselves. We free ourselves from the instinct that we cannot draw or paint which then gives our I Am the opportunity to express itself. Our I Am, after all, is the source of human talent. If we can get our lower self out of the way then our I Am has the opportunity to reveal our potential to make an image.

We could look at Easter images in this way and perhaps even draw them. Then we would experience our own resistance to being nailed to a cross in contrast to Jesus' willingness to do so.

In another instance, we may not like someone because we have a biased view of him or her. We disapprove of something we heard about this person. They then live in our soul in this biased way. If we met them and had a firsthand experience of them, we may have an entirely different view of them. Then we have the opportunity to sacrifice our bias and step over past-life memories to meet the person anew in this life.

Perhaps this is the sacrifice we must make about Christ Jesus. He is received with so much negativity that we struggle to make sense of the sacrificial deed of Golgotha. We can be deeply grateful for the work of Rudolf Steiner who resurrected the events so that we may bring them to life in our own souls.

In one such story, in the series published as Foundations of Esotericism, Steiner explains why Christ Jesus placed the sacrifice in the context of bread and wine, saying that they were his body and blood.

'What should develop in the future is a further ascent from plant to mineral nourishment. Bread and Wine must again be sacrificed, must be given up. Thus as Christ appeared in the Fourth Sub-Race he pointed to Bread and Wine: 'This is my Body; this is my Blood.' Here He wished to create a transition from animal nourishment to plant nourishment, the transition to something higher. ... "The significance of the Last Supper is the transition from nourishment taken from the dead animal to nourishment taken from the dead plant. When our Fifth Sub-Race will have reached its end, in the Sixth Sub-Race, the Last Supper will be understood. Even before this it will be possible for the third form of nourishment to begin to make its appearance, the purely mineral. Man himself will then be able to create his nourishment. Now he takes what the Gods have created for him. Later he will advance and will himself prepare in the chemical laboratory the substances he will require.

If such esoteric facts live in our soul, we will be able to sacrifice the natural, unconsciousness, state of our soul that can betray us. Then we become much more conscious of ourselves and of others. What follows next is that we sacrifice our lack of understanding and empathy for others, enabling us to share their experiences as if we were them. Entering into each other in this way is the I Am experience. It is our I Am that urges us to make the event of Golgotha a living experience because it was through the deed of Golgotha that we were given the possibility to have a personal connection with our I Am.

This essay was written around Easter 2009 which was the one hundredth anniversary of the approach of the etheric Christ as described by Steiner in his lectures in 1909. Robert Powell, during his visit to Australia in January 2009, suggested that this Easter will bring a very powerful in-streaming (*parousia*) of the Christ spirit.

Every Easter gives us the opportunity to create new images of the sacrifice of Christ. We should not worry about what images to make; if our efforts are motivated by a sincere striving to make Golgotha real, Christ will reveal himself to us through these images. We can stand with him and offer up our own sacrifices and in this way we become his co-worker. Then his presence in this world is revealed through us by our ability to stand in our own I Am.

First published in The Newsletter of the Anthroposophical Society In Australia, Victorian Branch Inc. Vol 25 No 1 Feb/March 2009

Christ - Sacrifice or Selfishness

Understanding Selfishness

We misunderstand the being of Christ if we think that he appeared on this earth without any preparation. In June 1914 Rudolf Steiner spoke of the four stages of preparation for Christ and for us.

The first one took place eons ago in the Lemurian period as the human race separated out of the ALL and began to assume its own individual physical presence. At the same time earth, plants and animals began to assume their own forms. It was only natural that selfishness arose for what was once within us was now outside us. We experienced the pain of separation. Lucifer tried to enhance this selfishness but Christ, ensouled in an Archangel, calmed our senses and helped us feel in harmony with what was now outside us.

This process of Christ imbued in an archangel was a similar process to what took place in the baptism of Jesus.

"In a kind of prefiguring of the John baptism, an archangel sacrificed his soul being to allow the Christ to imbue it; and by this means he released a power that worked into human evolution on earth." Quoted in "The Sufferings of the Nathan Soul" by Peter Selg*

From the same lecture are these awe inspiring words:

"The enjoyment of nature will be Christ-permeated [...] in the beauties of summer or other natural wonders, (people) will feel, and will say, that their delight in absorbing the impressions of natural beauty

around them must include an awareness that it is not them but Christ in their senses who endows them with the capacity to sense and perceive the glories of nature."

*The Sufferings of the Nathan Soul by Peter Selg or a different translation of the lecture "The Four Sacrifices of Christ" is available free on website rsarchive.com

The Purpose of Resisting Selfishness

There is a clear connection between selfishness and evil and they are part of our life for a purpose. Understanding this brings the freedom to achieve our highest potential. In his lecture "The Four Sacrifices of Christ" 1 June 1914, (mentioned above) Rudolf Steiner speaks of the astonishing story of Christ accompanying human development through all its stages. He urges us to be more aware of Christ and with deep gratitude to recognize that we could not live on this earth without him.

How do we feel when we make an important contribution that goes unrecognized? We could say this is egotistical, but is it? Perhaps it is preparing us to experience heartfelt gratitude for the being without whom we could not achieve our true destiny – for ourselves and for this Universe.

A second stage in Christ's journey to Golgotha involved his intervention in the activity of Lucifer and Ahriman who worked to make our vital organs selfish. Imagine the brain, heart, kidneys, liver and lungs fighting over who gets the most nutrients. Illness results, as Rudolf Steiner says,

"To be ill means that an organ has become selfish and is leading its own independent life within us."

We can only be healthy because of Christ's second sacrifice. Rudolf Steiner gives this example;

"when we picked cherries, for example, the related organ would have felt an inordinate greed. The human being would have felt, not the self-seeking organ only, but all the other organs also, striving against it with

equal selfishness!"

It is helpful if we create an Imagination of an Archangel offering up his soul powers to be permeated by the Christ. Then to *see "What was accomplished by this deed shining down into the earth's atmosphere. Then that harmonizing and balancing of the vital organs took place that rendered them selfless."*

It is only when we can use our will to create pictures, combining ideas through our thinking, then imbuing them feeling, that we will be able to say,

'in true piety, "I realize that I am able to exist as a physical man with unselfish organs because not I alone have developed myself in the world, but Christ in me, Who has so conditioned my organs that I can be a man!"'

These are wonderful ideas to contemplate as we try to understand what the presence of Christ in our life means.

Resisting Selfishness in our Soul Keeps us Sane

The third sacrifice Christ made on his journey into the body of Jesus took place in the last part of the Atlantean period when humanity faced a third danger. Lucifer and Ahriman intended to disturb our soul's activity by creating disorder in our thinking, feeling and willing. This meant that thinking, feeling and willing would not work harmoniously together, but each one would work independently and selfishly. How does this play out in our consciousness?

"Well, a person would have wished or willed something, would have pursued these will impulses, while his thinking pursued a different impulse, and his feeling yet another. [...] under the influence of Lucifer and Ahriman alone, thinking, feeling and will would have become egoistic, as it were, destroying the soul's harmonious action."

This means we would have been mentally disturbed, insane.

In my book "I Connecting" I describe how thinking, feeling and will work, giving practical advice about the ways in which we can keep these soul faculties in harmony.

"It is the will element that links or separates our thoughts. Feeling always permeates our thinking when we decide to like or dislike something. We experience feeling in our will when we are satisfied or dissatisfied with something we have done. Also, will plays through our feelings to give life to our thinking. If we think of walking the dog, it is not until our intentions are fired up with the warmth of feeling for the love of the dog and its wellbeing that our thought really comes to life. Otherwise it is just a thought and the dog won't have its walk." I Connecting by Kristina Kaine

Deep gratitude pours from us towards Christ when we truly understand that the possibility of the harmony of these faculties was gifted to us by him. A reminder of this act is found in the story of St George (or Archangel Michael) treading the dragon underfoot for bringing human thinking, feeling and will into disorder – and still does if we let him. As we pursue our spiritual development, we learn to harmonize thinking, feeling and will ourselves. We will do this more successfully if we acknowledge and love Christ for his third sacrifice.

Self-Sacrifice of Selfishness

At the next stage, Christ enters, not into an Archangel but into the human being known to us as Jesus of Nazareth. This sacrifice took place because Lucifer and Ahriman threatened to create confusion about the human 'I'. It is the 'I' that makes us human and gives us great power in the Cosmos. This, of course, is what Lucifer and Ahriman seek to undermine. Well, not so much undermine, but create a force of resistance that we must overcome.

"The 'I' could have failed to develop the capacity to retain its entity as self." as Rudolf Steiner put it. *"What comes from the soul would have been torn away by all elemental forces originating in wind, air and waves."*

Next time we stand on the coast during a weather event

we can imagine what this would be like.

We sometimes feel this disarray when we can't seem to 'pull ourselves together' to focus on things. This scattering can only be gathered together when we begin to experience something higher, the I Am which is our True Self; we can only come to this experience through Christ, there is no other way.

In our gratitude for the order Christ created by entering into the body of Jesus who was immobilized on the cross at Golgotha we join him. At the same time, we must feel connected to his pain, not from the nails in his hands and feet, but from the agony of entering into the human physical condition for the first time. In this way, he also had his first experience of fear. As we contemplate this event, it is not about focusing on crucifixion itself, but on its purpose for us.

This fourth sacrifice meant that:

"Human thinking, at risk before the advent of Christ, and redeemed by Christ's incarnation in its 'I'-informed and 'I'-governed order and clarity can and must seed our future evolution. The Christ impulse can enter and inform this thinking in so far as the human being succeeds in developing it further in a selfless, body-free way (pure thinking) and offering it up to the world of spirit and its revelations."

Our task is to feel deep gratitude to all the beings that brought us the gift which makes us fully human and fully divine. Especially on June 24 each year, at St John's Tide, we can be grateful to John the Baptist who was the only human being who could have heralded in the Cosmic Christ, often signified by the descending dove.

Palm Sunday

Riding the Ass

Palm Sunday is the doorway to the final steps taken by Christ Jesus to his crucifixion. To look deeply into this event we might need to scrape away all the mesmerizing and often trivial images the church has implanted into human minds over the centuries. Palm Sunday is not a story about an event in the life of a man who lived over 2,000 years ago; it is the story about what is happening within us now!

"And when they drew near to Jerusalem and came to Beth'phage, to the Mount of Olives, then Jesus sent two disciples, saying to them, "Go into the village opposite you, and immediately you will find an ass tied, and a colt with her; untie them and bring them to me. If any one says anything to you, you shall say, 'The Lord has need of them,' and he will send them immediately." This took place to fulfil what was spoken by the prophet, saying, "Tell the daughter of Zion, Behold, your king is coming to you, humble, and mounted on an ass, and on a colt, the foal of an ass." The disciples went and did as Jesus had directed them; they brought the ass and the colt, and put their garments on them, and he sat thereon. Most of the crowd spread their garments on the road, and others cut branches from the trees and spread them on the road. And the crowds that went before him and that followed him shouted, "Hosanna to the Son of David! Blessed is he who comes in the name of the Lord! Hosanna in the highest!" And when he entered Jerusalem, all the city was stirred, saying, 'Who is this?'" Matthew 21:1-10

This ass and its colt have not just been tied up, they have been bound; the Greek word is *deo,* which means tightly bound, perhaps in chains. These animals represent our animal nature, our astral or earthly ego, which often behaves like an ass. This is the seat of our emotions, our feelings, our sympathy and antipathy, and it can have a paralyzing and polarizing effect on us.

If we are to develop our spiritual nature then we must tie up our animal nature, we must bind it strongly so that it cannot work against us. We find this animal nature in our instincts, in fact, in all our behavior that is animal-like. This is the part of us called our astral body or astral being and it is here that we find the human ego. The ego is an important part of us because it essentially ensures that we prevail. We live in a society where everyone is striving to prevail. Mostly we are unaware of this until we are in a situation where one person has the opportunity to go first, or get something before us, or be chosen ahead of us, and so on. Then the ego steps up and says, "Pick me!"

So the ego has ensured our survival but at some point we must have the experience that we have now prevailed, that we have focused on ourselves sufficiently and now something higher begins to operate. Then we bind the ass and any offspring it may have. This binding represents the end of a cycle in our development.

When we are ready to proceed we can unbind the ass, which is like the symbol of a spiral, it changes from the inwards turning to the outwards turning. Then we ride on it. We demonstrate that we have conquered our animal nature, our astral – which has been so necessary in carrying us thus far in our development. This ass and its colt now have a higher function; when they are conquered in our physical being, they can then operate in our spiritual being as Imagination. They then represent the depth of feeling we can have when we create images in our mind to bring to life the true concepts of human nature which in the highest is our I AM. *"Blessed is he who comes in the name of the Lord!"* Lord is the *kurios* which means our I AM.

Jesus Entering Jerusalem

As with all the events in the Bible, we can look at them from different angles. Palm Sunday marks the beginning of the final phase of the journey for Jesus as he fully assumes the Cosmic Christ force into himself when he is crucified. We have so little understanding of the power of this force. If we received it into ourselves unprepared it could blow us apart. This, of course, must not happen and we can look to sacred texts for guidance about how we might participate of this force without damaging ourselves.

The next day a great crowd who had come to the feast heard that

Jesus was coming to Jerusalem. So they took branches of palm trees and went out to meet him, crying, "Hosanna! Blessed is he who comes in the name of the Lord, even the King of Israel!" And Jesus found a young ass and sat upon it; as it is written, "Fear not, daughter of Zion; behold, your king is coming, sitting on an ass's colt!" John 12:12-15

We can observe this event in our Imagination and see the crowd taking the branches – were they dead ones that had fallen or did someone scale these giant palms and cut fresh green ones? They would have needed a lot for a crowd. Would it have been easier for the ass to walk on these branches? Probably not. These are the details that we can think about to bring these stories to life. While this describes an outer event, it also happens within us.

Imagine many young men quickly scaling the mighty Palm trees whose fronds seems to reach up and touch the sun. It was as if they were bringing down the very sunlight itself to pave the way for Jesus. He is the Lord, the I AM, and it was the divine purpose of the nation of Israel produce a pure bloodline that could contain the very presence of the Cosmic Christ.

The ass represents our animal or instinctive astral nature, which can be very unruly. Our I AM must ride on the forces of our astral body into Jerusalem - the place of peace which is acquired by repeated effort. Only when we have done this work in our soul, by becoming aware of the activity of our thoughts, feelings and intentions, will our soul become the daughter of Zion, elevated. Then we can begin to experience the presence of Christ within us. However, the soul always likes to know that it is supported by the astral when we can feel as if the ground beneath us no longer supports us. Then we can look towards the king, the Christen-ed I AM and know that we have fully prepared ourselves for the journey through Holy Week.

Palm Sunday and our Guardian Angel

If we walk through the weeks of Lent with purpose it can assist us to have a genuine experience of our Guardian Angel. This relationship is not static; it changes as we develop our understanding of the spiritual world. This spiritual world is not 'up there' we live in it; it is all around us and in us. We don't see it because its physical manifestation distracts our attention.

How would this world appear if the spiritual world in which we live divested itself of its physical sheath? What would we see if the physical world disappeared from view? We would see all the spiritual activity that sustains the earth, the vegetation, the animals, and human beings. We would also see the activity of the angels as the messengers, Gk angelos, of the Cosmos who communicate earthly events to higher beings, while at the same time making themselves available to communication Cosmic events to us if we are willing to hear them.

In our journey through Lent, we eventually reach Palm Sunday and in this story we find each of the four elements; the dusty earth, the etheric palm leaves, the astral donkey, and Jesus who represents the highest earthly expression of humanity, the I Am. It is the I Am that is able to subdue the animal that has never been ridden – that is its task now.

Palm Sunday tells us that our astral (animal) has never been ridden by a human I Am – think about what it takes to break-in a horse or a donkey. Angels are connected to the astral (starry) worlds and hence with the forces of our astral body which means that they will help us break-in our astral. They won't do it for us but if we show signs of willingness to do the work they will assist us all the way. This gives us a very strong motive to have a real relationship with our Guardian Angel.

5 THE CRUCIFIXION AND RESURRECTION

How to Stay Conscious at Easter

The reason for Easter can raise many questions. We see a man nailed to a cross saying some very interesting – perhaps strange – things that we can filter through the limits of our understanding. We can drown in the detail, or we can contemplate one aspect of it to bring it to life in our consciousness. Will we see Jesus; the man, the blood, the pain, the desertion, the despair? Or will we see the mighty spiritual being we call Christ entering into the very bones of this man and experiencing death firsthand and for the first time?

Why? Purely and simply so that every human being in the Universe could become like him. What is it like to become like him? Eternal, I Am, spiritual-physical, first of all consciously in our mind. We can only do this if we think the thoughts that awaken us to the reality that we are much greater than our awareness reveals to us. To be bigger than we are is to embrace each other, embrace our differences, to love, to forgive, to enter into each other with deep compassion. We do this with our spirit as we tame our soul's automatic responses.

What is this spirit? It is a Holy Spirit, a whole Spirit. Our Whole Spirit awareness comes about through a tamed soul. What is an untamed soul? One that reacts to karma, one that lazily participates in modern jargon, one that believes they are right and particularly one that is polarized by likes and dislikes.

Our task is to find our Holy or Whole Spirit and there is no better time than during Lent to prepare for the post-Easter event. If we contemplate the purpose of Easter, it can become clear to us that we participate in this cosmic event each year as Cosmic beings, not just the person we are in this incarnation.

We have a role to play and that role is to awaken our Whole Spirit – not just for us but for the whole Universe.

This quote by Sergei Prokofieff is helpful.

In the lecture of 30 July 1922 (GA 214) we find a detailed description of the fact that Christ, who is an all-encompassing cosmic being and enters directly into man's inner nature, would have inevitably extinguished all trace of individual ego-consciousness if He had not sent the Holy Spirit, who has since Pentecost enabled Him to dwell in every human ego without extinguishing its consciousness. Note 23 Part VIII The Mystery of Pentecost, in The Cycle of the Year by Sergei Prokofieff

The word 'sent' means to come from one place to another and this can mean from our soul to our spirit. We can therefore rephrase the words, "if He had not sent the Holy Spirit" in this way: 'if He had not given us the possibility of connecting with our Whole Spirit using our earthly consciousness [our earthly consciousness would be extinguished].' This is the purpose of Easter.

The Real Purpose of the Resurrection

How well do we understand the Resurrection? What does it mean to say, "He is risen!"? If Jesus resurrected, where is he now? Or was it Christ who resurrected? Or something else?

Understanding the life of Jesus and his connection with the Christ raises more questions than answers, or at least it should. Asking the questions opens our minds to new possibilities. Thinking we have the answer will only close us off to truth. Truth is a slippery thing anyway. If we are open to it, we can reach an understanding one day, and on another day have a much greater understanding of the same truth. Isn't this a resurrection? A resurrection of understanding!

What if our ability to resurrect our understanding is a direct result of the resurrection experienced by Christ! That would be significant. It is true that something happened in human evolution at the time Christ was crucified and then went through the resurrection. Could it be that this event made it possible for human beings to understand the mysteries differently? Prior to the Christ event, as already mentioned, only those who were initiated had access to higher knowledge. When Jesus went through the crucifixion allowing the Christ Spirit to enter fully into his human body, every human body changed forever.

The Life-Force

What changed we can ask? The life-force in our body was renewed. Why? Because it was becoming depleted of the life it had since it took on the body of flesh described in the Adam and Eve event. A bit further on in this book you will come to an essay called "Have You Seen Christ Jesus? Did It Happen Like This?" where this force is described as *"the etheric life-force in all living things. In our body it is the force that opposes the decay of our physical substance. When this force loses its principle of opposition, our physical bodies die."*

What does it mean for us to know that our life-force has

been renewed? A lot, actually! For instance, it means that when we die, this life-force is preserved to some extent, it doesn't completely dissolve as it used to in the past. This means that now something of us remains after death. To know what remains we need to understand what this life-force, this etheric body, does while we live.

Primarily it is connected to memory. When we think our thoughts and commit them to memory these memories are stored in our etheric body. This means that when we die our ideas continue, not as they were while we lived, but now in a new way, as if they acquire new life. It sounds like a living library of ideas, and it is.

Rudolf Steiner says,

"For Goethe's way of thinking has been transformed and lives on in a different form. It is important that we should grasp Christianity in the same spirit."

This is how it works. One person develops a deep understanding of a topic, but during their life they cannot express it fully, their understanding is limited by their physical body. When they die the full expression endures and when another person studies the same ideas they can draw on the thoughts of the previous person preserved in the etheric life-force of the world and develop these ideas further.

"Once you have had the experience of having been in touch with the thoughts of someone who has died, whose physical body has been committed to the earth and whose thoughts live on in you, then a time comes when you say: 'The thoughts that have newly arisen in me I owe to Christ; they could never have become so vitally alive but for the incarnation of Christ.'"

The same applies to anything we study, the Bible or any sacred writing as well as the works of Rudolf Steiner and other spiritual teachers. The way they were written down and understood in one era can be further developed later on, resurrected in a new form. The Christen-ed Jesus made this possible.

As Rudolf Steiner said,

"It is not a question of invoking incessantly the name of the Lord; what matters is that we grasp the living spirit of Christianity, that we hold fast to the vitally important idea of resurrection as a living force."

Quotes from "Building Stones for an Understanding of the Mystery of Golgotha" Lecture 8, April 24, 1917

What is Crucified? What is Resurrected?

In preparation for Easter each year we can walk through Lent with Angels. Each time we contemplate the Angels, and especially our own Guardian Angel, they draw near to us. They want to help us understand a greater reality but they never interfere with our own efforts to do so.

So, how much do we know about Easter? After we remove the graphic images of rabbits and eggs what are we left with? Since I am predominately writing about human consciousness, I am drawn to the ideas that are revealed when we look at the nature of the human soul and its relationship to the I Am. How exactly do we discover truth?

All knowledge is hidden in the depths of our soul. The big question is how to access this knowledge. The events of Easter show us how. In chapter 4 of his seminal work, "Theosophy," Rudolf Steiner explains how we can access this knowledge.

"It is in the very assimilating of the communications of others that the first step [and further steps] towards personal knowledge consists. [...] all knowledge of the worlds of soul and spirit slumbers in the profoundest depths of the human soul. [...] Correct spiritual insight awakens the power of comprehension in anyone whose inner nature is not beclouded by preconceptions and prejudices." I encourage you to read the whole chapter available on line at the rsarchive.com.

Hold onto these ideas and consider this. At Easter, what is crucified? And, what is resurrected?

The deep Easter message is that earthly thinking tainted by lazy, subconscious sensations and feelings must die. More often than not, we are unaware of the level of what I call psychic sensations cloud our thinking.

What is resurrected? Living thinking, thinking filled with good will, which is gentle will. This thinking can look intently at information and wait patiently until it reveals its inner nature. Then, sustained by this living thinking, we can apply these new meanings to our own lives. This thinking is sharp and clear, never abstract or biased, and the ideas it reveals transform us, transubstantiate us; change our body and blood into a new substance capable of awakening a new "power of comprehension."

How to Engage in Our Own Resurrection Process

After Easter we enter into the process of Resurrection which lasts for 40 days until Ascension and then 10 days later we reach the very important time of Pentecost. The effort we put in is rewarded at Pentecost.

Our challenge is to pull ourselves away from the ideas taught by the church over centuries, and enter into the deeper meaning of the Easter events for the evolution of our own consciousness. Too much focus on God or Jesus comes at the expense of valuing our own contribution to human development.

The post Easter period is sometimes referred to as the Mystical Interval, suggesting a period of rest after the traumatic Easter event. This is far from the case. We have important work to do in the weeks between Easter and Pentecost so that we, and this whole universe, benefit as much as possible at Pentecost.

Easter culminated with Christ entering into the physical body of Jesus and there, for the first time, experiencing fully the way the spirit of this world has been clothed in physical matter. This is such a powerful idea, but what it is really saying is that Christ, the world I AM, entered into the physical body of Jesus, the human aspect of the I Am, and there, for the first time, experienced the world of the physical senses; spirit that has put on the cloak of physical matter. Not only that but also he experienced the human ability to think, which is a god-like quality.

Rising Out of the Body

Then he arose out of the body of Jesus forever changed. We must do the same – not physically but in our consciousness. We nail our earthly thinking to the cross and we arise in a new kind of thinking that is not bound to the images of the senses. We haven't done this if we still only see the cruelty of Jesus nailed to the cross.

Only with disciplined thinking can we experience its resurrection as the new clairvoyance. Unfortunately, what tends to happen at this point of resurrection, when we begin to see spiritual reality, we drop thinking and enter into an unconscious feeling process that is undisciplined clairvoyance.

How do we avoid this? It all depends on our connection with our own I Am as well as the world I AM. It is through our I Am that we develop the strong power of thinking, and to the degree that we achieve this, the world I AM assists us. We then bring this connection into the spiritual world where we retain the sense of our own individuality instead of being swallowed up in the undifferentiated ALL. If we cannot maintain this sense of self, spiritual beings can enter into our consciousness which results in seductive undisciplined clairvoyance.

Where can we start? We can start by loving others, truly loving others free of any personal motives. This true love enters into others and experiences them as if they were ourselves. Out of this experience arises deep respect and understanding for the personal journey each of us must make.

That is resurrection.

Experiencing the Resurrection Process Everywhere in our Lives

What is it really like to die, to pass through the grave, and then to experience the resurrection? These processes of death, burial, and resurrection are an integral part of our lives. They happen every day all around us in a myriad of ways. Mostly we don't notice them except if a family member or friend dies. Even then, we only focus on the death part of the process.

As we contemplate the resurrection, it could be helpful to be more aware of other death-burial-resurrection processes in our lives. It happens in nature, in our relationships, in our work processes and even in our digestion, and more. It is not hard to see these three processes taking place in nature; it takes a little more effort to see them in our relationships and work. Our relationships would not survive without the death-burial-resurrection process, and this is why they sometimes break down because those involved become stuck in one or the other stage. In digestion, our food is killed in our stomach by the gastric enzymes, buried in our intestines, and resurrected in our blood.

We could even say that the whole purpose of the crucifixion, burial, and resurrection of Christ Jesus was to put these three processes front and center for all human beings. Not only that, the human race is going through this same process in a broader evolutionary context. We died to the spiritual worlds when we took on human form; we are buried in this physical world; and we have commenced the resurrection process.

This resurrection process is a personal journey and it is up to us to engage with it. Although, thank goodness, our digestion is not up to us, and it is possible that if we consume food without the right attitude, this may result in damage to our body. The breakdown in friendships, and in interest groups, is certainly due to the unwillingness to move forward into the new.

The resurrection is a powerful image of hope as we pass through the greatest period of darkness that humanity has ever experienced. How incredible that a mighty God called Christ struggled to enter into a body of matter, having no idea what it was like, just so that we could find our way out of the darkness in which we currently live!

If we don't understand the images this builds in our minds then the crucifixion and resurrection happened in vain. In fact, the crucifixion and resurrection are continuous processes taking place in the spiritual worlds until humanity gets it!

Have you Seen Christ Jesus? Did it Happen Like This?

When we look into the details of the Christ being and the life of Jesus it is understandable to ask why is the Christ Being is so misunderstood. Perhaps it is a frightening idea that one great Cosmic Being is within us and around us seeking to unite us all in a community of loving individuals. Is this picture too big for us to comprehend? Do we actually prefer to stay in small cliques of agreeable people and ostracize anyone who disrupts the status quo? In the text below, Jesus tells the people to go to Galilee, the place of mixed races and creeds.

We should also take into account that many people speak about God out there somewhere who they can pray to when they experience difficulties. But even then they want to compartmentalize this God and tie him to different belief systems.

Should we be concerned about all this unbelief? For that is what it is, we can't call it belief because there are so many things people don't believe in. It is not only their unbelief, it is also the way they work around the ideas that make them comfortable or uncomfortable. Let's have a look at what Matthew writes about the Risen Christ.

"And behold, Jesus met them and said, "Hail!" And they came up and took hold of his feet and worshiped him. Then Jesus said to them, "Do not be afraid; go and tell my brethren to go to Galilee, and there they will see me." While they were going, behold, some of the guard went into the city and told the chief priests all that had taken place. And when they had assembled with the elders and taken counsel, they gave a sum of money to the soldiers and said, "Tell people, 'His disciples came by night and stole him away while we were asleep.' And if this comes to the governor's ears, we will satisfy him and keep you out of trouble." So they took the money and did as they were directed; and this story has been spread among the Jews to this day." Matthew 28:9-15

Let's begin by exploring the true meaning of some of the words in this text. *"Behold"*, *idou*, has a special meaning indicating an all-encompassing perception. You don't just see physical forms; you see and know everything about what you are seeing.

"Jesus met them"; met is *hypantao*, which means a confrontation. It suggests a certain level of force - not a friendly force but an opposing force. This opposing force is the etheric life-force in all living things. In our bodies it is the force that opposes the decay of our physical substance. When this force loses its principle of opposition, our physical bodies die.

Since Jesus' body has disappeared, it is from this force that Jesus said, *"Hail."* Hail is *chairo*, which also means rejoice. Using our imagination we can see a mighty spiritual being, an imposing and frightening etheric figure greeting the people in a way that draws them to him - drawn in the way we are drawn to nature. Nature is especially etheric.

"And they came up and took hold of his feet and worshiped him." *"They came up"* is *proserchomai; pros* means moving towards, and *erchomi* is a very specific word which means to come from one place to another, to change position, not just physically. This

suggests that these people entered into a spiritual connection with Jesus. As they physically stand there, they move to spiritually connect with him.

"Took hold of", is *krateo*, which means to have power, and refers to the Spiritual Hierarchy of Exousia, named Elohim in the Hebrew language, also referred to in the Bible as Powers. These are the Creator Gods spoken of in the first verse in Genesis who created this physical world and, as intermediaries, hold and herald the power of the Cosmic Christ.

Feet *podas* could mean just that part of him which was approachable from the lower etheric levels. It is interesting that they were not warned not to touch him as Mary was in St John's Gospel, "Jesus said to her, *'Do not hold me.'"* Jn 20:17. Perhaps enough time had passed that this mighty etheric presence was anchored in the spiritual world and supported by all the beings in the Spiritual Hierarchy.

Of course they worshiped him. Worshiped is *proskyneo,* and means 'to kiss towards' and indicates reverence.

The Etheric Experience

We are left with the impression of an extremely powerful event. One in which we are shaken free of our earthly body enabling us to be present in our etheric body and there to meet the Risen Christ in his etheric body. It would be frightening; it would feel like the ground beneath our feet has fallen away. Yet we don't feel unsupported, we replace our feet with his feet, we *"take hold of his feet"* giving us a feeling of security and reverence.

This is a description of what will happen to us when we perceive the living Christ. Of course we will be shaken. It will be like no other experience we have ever had. The physical world in which we have been living will lose its value - or at least the value we have given it. We will now see it for what it is; a stage in the process of standing in our own I Am.

When we perceive the living Christ we will be stirred to reverence and we will be called to act - *"go to Galilee"*. This is because Christ is not to be found in the church, he is in the world, and he disturbs us. Then Jesus said to them, *"Do not be afraid; go and tell my brethren to go to Galilee, and there they will see me."*

"Go and tell" really says 'take word' *apangello; apo*, means a state of separation, and *angelos*, means angels, messengers, supporting the idea that this is a spiritual event. *"There they will see"* where 'see' is *horao* which means to see what appears. What appears is the etheric Christ, divested of his physical substance, which they will see.

What takes place between the guard, the chief priests, the elders, and soldiers is the perfect description of today's society. The truth is silenced and money is elevated to a Christ-like position. Nothing is more valuable in the world today, or more worshipped than money. Lies are told to support this position which prevents us from seeing the etheric presence of Christ who is waiting for us to reach up and to hold his feet with reverence. Quoted from "Who is Jesus : What is Christ?" Vol 5 by Kristina Kaine

Christ is in me - but Where?

"The Christ we seek is within us, in our inmost self, is our inmost self, and yet infinitely transcends ourselves." Thomas Merton, citing a letter to D.T. Suzuki, 1959.

When I read quotes and statements like this I am left wondering what to do with it. It is as if I have nothing to hang on to - Christ in me, but where? It is no longer appropriate to blindly take statements like this - perhaps out of context although I wonder about that. I do not doubt the truth of the statement, far from it, but I need to be able to think it through in more detail. If I am going to make some bread I need some understanding of the role the ingredients play otherwise I will end up with a flour brick instead of lovely soft and fluffy bread.

So how do I find the Christ within me? If I go to the Bible and look deeply into a text similar to the statement:

"But if Christ is in you, although your bodies (soma) are dead because of sin, your spirits are alive (zoe) because of righteousness." Romans 8:10

If Christ is in you, your astral *soma* dies because you miss the mark *harmatia* which means sin and your etheric life force *zoe* is spiritualized *pneuma* because you have balanced and impartial thinking *dikaiosune* - righteousness. Then Paul goes on to say that our astral is raised from the dead.

So Christ is a raising agent (perhaps this is why he said "I am the bread"). He is within us and he assists us to transcend our astral tendencies, which are self-centered, egotistical. He helps us to balance our feeling, thinking and will so that we am not absorbed with worry about situations in our life, consumed with anger when someone upsets us, or act without thought and punch someone on the nose. These are sins; these are unbalanced, instinctive responses to life that are far, far away from the goal we are aiming for. If we can hold our instinctive responses at bay just for a moment we "transcend ourselves" and immediately feel free - that is the experience of Christ within us.

Do we Hear Christ Speaking to us?

It is interesting to contemplate that the Bible is the most popular book in the world. If more homes have a Bible than any other book, is the Bible read? If it is read, is it really understood? Sacred texts are living words requiring that we enter into them with respect and with openness, and most of all with love. If we contemplate a text with such reverence it will speak to us of many things.

If we place ourselves into the story by creating the scene in our imagination, the story can come to life within us. We can stand in the story and look around, play the roles of the different people, hear the words as if they are being spoken to us or by us and so on. Some of the most powerful texts to do this with are those that report the appearance of Christ after the crucifixion. They are stories of the risen Christ speaking to his people. This Christ is a real presence, not a physical presence, but appearing in his spiritualized physical body which is enlivened by his pure life-force. This life-force, his pure etheric force, is that force which keeps us alive as long as it is connected with us, and causes us to die if it leaves us. We need to create imaginations of this too.

After the crucifixion the risen Christ spoke to Mary outside the tomb (John 20:15-17), to the disciples on several occasions (John 20 and 21) and to Paul on his way to Damascus (Acts 9). In Acts 9 we read the amazing story of Paul's encounter with the risen Christ. Paul's mind was overflowing with hatred and he was consumed with thoughts of ways to destroy Christ's followers, when suddenly a light shone around him. It was such a mighty light that Paul was over-powered and sank to the ground. We can visualize this without too much effort.

St Paul's Experience

It was not the light which physics describes but the light that shines when higher realms of experience are opened to mankind. It was more than the radiance we emit from our soul when we experience spiritual truth, more than a mere mingling with the astral realms, but a breaking into the realm where Light itself originates. The light of the outer world is but a feeble reflection of it. The Light that Paul perceived is a Light of untold power, and it is at the same time utmost purity, radiant holiness, and divine wisdom.

Christ is there, and fills the being of Paul for a moment with the majesty and glory of Light. He cannot remain upright in this irradiation.

Out of the Light came a voice, breaking in upon him from every side: "Saul! Saul! Why are you persecuting me?" Such voices come not only from outside us but also from within us at the same time. They are not audible to the outer ear; it is as though we spoke the words ourselves, and yet we didn't but the echo of them is there.

The words of Christ were heard by Paul in his true being, in that part of him that has waited longingly in the depths of his heart for the presence of Christ to stir, and is now he is called by Christ. Like a hero it comes forth out of its chamber. Paul says. "Lord, what will you have me do?" This is Paul the crusader for Christ who speaks. Paul who later says from firsthand experience, "Not I, but Christ in me", Paul who is determined to know nothing but Christ crucified and risen again. The man of will in Paul begins to stir and all the hours of his life from now on work out of this hour. This hour that Paul experienced stands before us all. If it doesn't come within our earthly life, we can meet it at the moment of our death.

The Power of Christ's Word

The words Christ speaks to Paul - and he speaks them to us too - are born from within the soul. If we hear them, like Paul, we experience the freedom in our I Am as well as union with the I AM of Christ in exquisite harmony. Such harmony as this creates music in the Cosmos for all those beings who longingly await this moment of human hearing.

Christ calls to us in every word that He spoke, can we hear him? Within every word of His lives the whole experience of Paul at Damascus if we dare to enter into them with the highest and most pure love.

Pause for a moment and think about this.

When we hear one of the great words of Christ, in the moment it lives within us a new world of Light dawns within us. It is not the single experience that we may have from the word that is important; through the word a divine Light sheds its rays upon us and the divine World draws near to us. We are amazed again and again at the fullness of Light that is 'imprisoned' in Christ's word; Light that waits for whomever is ready to receive it. Then we realize that the Kingdom of Christ is here on Earth – in His words.

Like Paul we can say, "Lord what will you have me do?" The courage of our I Am speaks. We recognize that the 'I' of Christ is the secret lying in the depths of every word He spoke. This Christed 'I' can come to us again when we bring to mind his words as they have been faithfully recorded in the Gospels.

The men of old would have said: "A Christ initiation awaits us in every word of Christ."

- o Our thinking, our spirit, receives the Light of Christ – and our whole life is different when we turn upon it the Christ Light from one of His words.

- o Our feeling, our soul, receives the Nature and Being of Christ – although at first in such a way that it feels its own distance from Him.

- o Our will, our physical being, receives the Will of Christ – and a new world of transformation opens up within it.

Again, pause and think this through. Apply these ideas to the different areas of body, soul, and spirit.

Know Yourself!

As we strive towards self-knowledge in response to the ancient cry "Human Being, know yourself!" our spiritual understanding of ourselves deepens and we begin to become more aware of the darkness in our being: our selfish inclinations, the real impetus behind our motives, our fears and so on. Memories from past lives begin to surface and we find ourselves confronting people who we have offended in a past life in some way or other. We become aware of a strained relationship but we are not fully consciousness of the details. We can experience anxiety, fear, and dread, among other things. On the other hand, we may find that a person acts towards us in a strange way and we can feel offended wondering what we have done to deserve being treated in this way.

While we live through such difficulties without fully knowing what is behind them we need to develop ways of coping. Superficial methods like positive thinking are not appropriate, for these experiences are there for a purpose. They are there to give us the opportunity to resolve past life deeds through the agency of our Higher Self, our I Am. In this way we integrate our I Am into our being. If we deal with issues through our lower self which is tied to our astral, self-protection and egotism will shut out our I Am and nothing will be resolved.

How to Stay Calm

One way to prepare us to deal with such issues in a mature way is to use events in the Bible to calm our fear and to become the objective observer. We should avoid at all costs being too distant from what is happening, after all, it is happening for our own benefit. We can become what I call *The Interested Observer*. This calms down our reactions and assists us to see what lies beneath the surface of events (and what lies beneath the surface is what is esoteric).

Here is one method to calm down. Read this text and place yourself in the story.

"On the evening of that day, the first day of the week, the doors being shut where the disciples were, for fear of the Jews, Jesus came and stood among them and said to them, "Peace be with you." When he had said this, he showed them his hands and his side. Then the disciples were glad when they saw the Lord. Jesus said to them again, "Peace be with you. As the Father has sent me, even so I send you." And when he had said this, he breathed on them, and said to them, "Receive the Holy Spirit. If you forgive the sins of any, they are forgiven; if you retain the sins of any, they are retained." John 20:19-23

Here we have the story of what happened to the disciples after Jesus was crucified. They were so afraid they couldn't even attend the event. They locked themselves in a room and the next thing they knew Jesus stood among them – he didn't use the door, it was locked. Think about the level of fear they would have experienced. They had deserted him in his final hour and now he had come to find them.

Then hear Jesus saying "Peace be with you." Try to make these words as real as possible in your mind.

Now place this story within you. The upper room is your head; the disciples are all your different thoughts and attitudes. Imagine the light associated with the presence of Jesus, who has just received into himself the fullness of the Cosmic Christ, standing among all your thoughts and feelings. Then hear the words, "Peace be with you." Feel your anxiety and fear subside, feel peaceful, and feel the movement of the breath of the Holy Spirit restoring balance and objectivity within your mind.

If you practice this Imaginative experience you will be able to call it into action at will whenever there is alarm in our soul.

Finally, read the following text imaginatively as if it is taking place within you.

Now Thomas, one of the twelve, called the Twin, was not with them when Jesus came. So the other disciples told him, "We have seen the Lord." But he said to them, "Unless I see in his hands the print of the nails, and place my finger in the mark of the nails, and place my hand in his side, I will not believe." Eight days later, his disciples were again in the house, and Thomas was with them. The doors were shut, but Jesus came and stood among them, and said, "Peace be with you." Then he said to Thomas, "Put your finger here, and see my hands; and put out your hand, and place it in my side; do not be faithless, but believing." Thomas answered him, "My Lord and my God!" Jesus said to him, "Have you believed because you have seen me? Blessed are those who have not seen and yet believe." Now Jesus did many other signs in the presence of the disciples, which are not written in this book; but these are written that you may believe that Jesus is the Christ, the Son of God, and that believing you may have life in his name." John 20:19-31

As an afterthought: When we hear people say something like, "Jesus came to take away the sins of the world." He didn't come to do our work for us, he came to assist us to do our own work.

Speak to Christ, He will Answer

Many of us struggle to understand the troubling times we live in. It seems that every kind of violence is not only escalating but it is more brazen. What are we to make of this?

One thing is for sure, we should not respond with fear and judgment. Compassion and love are called for, always mindful that the King and Shepherd of this world is guiding us forward. Why is he doing in this way? Well, as Rudolf Steiner explains, we should ask him.

"Why do we study spiritual science [Anthroposophy]? We do it to learn the vocabulary that we need to draw closer to Christ. [...] we need to learn to find in that language the questions we can address to the Christ. He will answer; yes, he will answer!" Rudolf Steiner, Building Stones for an Understanding of the Mystery of Golgotha

Does Jesus Save us?

After exploring the events of Jesus and Christ let's look a bit more into the role of Jesus.

Jesus is regularly referred to as a savior. Mainstream churches use the catch-cry, "Jesus Saves". Really! What does he save? Some say, "He saves me from my sins." I cannot believe that every time I sin Jesus will save me – and everyone else who is sinning. What would be the point of that! What would we learn from it – it seems to me that when people say that, they are not really thinking it through.

If I have learnt anything about the Bible, it is that every

single word makes an important point. The Bible is so clever that no translator has been able to interfere with the real meaning. So what is the true meaning of describing Jesus as a savior?

The idea of Jesus saving is first mentioned in the New Testament in Matthew chapter 1, when the Angel announces the birth of Jesus to Joseph.

"... she will bear a son, and you shall call his name Jesus, for he will save his people from their sins." Matthew 1:20-21

The meaning of the name Jesus is savior or deliverer. The question to ask is does the savior do the actual saving? A deliverer simply takes something from one place to another. It seems to me that we must save ourselves which is now made easier because Christ was able to unite himself with this earth; in fact, Jesus delivered him here!

We might be able to make more sense of this if we understand the word 'sin' - see the essay about sin further on. The Greek word for sin is *hamartion* and means 'to miss the mark'. Imagine if we had a quiver full of arrows and these arrows represented our thoughts: how often would we hit the mark because our thoughts were true? We must admit that, left to our own devices, we don't know what to think about certain things. There are many things in this world that we don't understand and therefore can't form thoughts about them. This is especially true of things that are new.

Essentially, the birth of Jesus heralded in a new era of human consciousness. Unless we understand that human consciousness changes we cannot understand the significance of the birth of Jesus, or the crucifixion of Jesus enabling him to receive the Christ Spirit into himself fully, and then the subsequent resurrection.

In a nutshell, before Christ (BC) we didn't think our own thoughts. Whatever thoughts we had were instinctual and dependent on the guidance of the tribal leader. We did not have the ability to make our own concepts from all that we saw in our environment. This instinctive process began to fade away and we started being able to put two and two together in our own minds, a process that has reached its zenith in present day sciences.

Now many scientists are admitting that they see concepts that are beyond their ability to prove. We could say that a higher instinct is entering into human consciousness, but this time it must be thought through. We could call this awareness higher imagining, higher inspiration, and higher intuition. These three represent (in order) our ability to create pictures from our own ideas, to hear new ideas echoing within us, and to experience something new so that we know it intimately. Many people who invent things will tell us that this is how they came to understand their invention in the first place.

So the term "Jesus Saves!" doesn't mean that we can sit back and hand over responsibility to him. It means that we must understand what he did, as well as the implication of his deed for our consciousness. We could say that Jesus has saved us from the abyss between the death of unthinking instincts by instigating the birth of these higher faculties of picturing, hearing and experiencing beyond what physically meets our senses.

The Power of the Presence of Christ

Apart from all the wonderful experiences my teacher Rev Mario Schoenmaker (1929-1997) gave me of the presence of Christ, it was Prokofieff in "The Cycle of the Year" who drew my attention anew to the voice of Christ in 1999. As I read Prokofieff's words, *"... await the moment when we shall find those questions which we may address to Christ. And He will answer. Yes, He will answer!"* I felt that my relationship with Christ reached a new level.

Then in 2002 I found a dilapidated copy of "The Holy Year" meditations in the Steiner Bookshop Library written by Friedrich Rittelmeyer (1872-1938) who was a leading figure in the Lutheran Church at the beginning of the 20th century. In 1922 he sacrificed an eminent position to lead The Christian Community, a movement for religious renewal founded with the co-operation of Rudolf Steiner.

While reading Rittelmeyer's "The Holy Year" and his "Meditation, Guidance for the Inner Life" I taught myself to see Christ standing before me and speaking any of the words he speaks in the Bible, as if he is saying the same words now, today, and to me. If I become anxious, I see Christ standing right in front of me and speaking directly to me, "Peace be with you" and my anxiety melts away and is replaced by the thrill of the presence of Christ.

6 WHO OR WHAT IS GOD?

Exploring the Nature of God

One of the most difficult things in the Bible to unlock is the understanding of God. The most astounding thing I heard when I began to really study the Bible was that there were many gods. Not in the sense of the ancient Greeks and Romans looking towards Olympus - although that could hold some answers as well - but in the sense that the Highest God needs other mighty beings to implement His intentions.

Take for instance the first words in the Bible,

"In the beginning God created the heavens and the earth."

In Hebrew this text says,

"Bereshit bara Elohim et hashamayim ve'et ha'arets."

The word translated into English as God is Elohim. Who is this Elohim character? For the Hebrews God was Jehovah or YHVH, but they also had other gods, described in

Wikipedia in this way:

El Elyon ("Most High God"), *El Shaddai* ("God Almighty"), *El 'Olam* ("Everlasting God"), *El Hai* ("Living God"), *El Ro'i* ("God of Seeing"), *El Elohe Israel* ("God, the God of Israel"), *El Gibbor* ("God of Strength")

It will be no accident that there are seven. Then there is Moses' famous conversation with God at the burning bush, when Moses asks God what his name is (Exodus 3:14) and the response is *Ehyeh asher ehyeh,* I am that I am. In the New Testament, Jesus refers to this I Am often using the Greek words *ego eimi.* Notably when he was challenged about where his authority came from, John records his response:

"Very truly I tell you," Jesus answered, "before Abraham was born, I am!" John 8:58

Understanding the I Am can provide answers to questions we may have about God.

Amidst all this confusion, it is perfectly understandable when people say, "I don't believe in God." They have the courage to admit that, so far, they have no information to assist them to have any plausible understanding of God. Blind faith doesn't do it. When they come across ideas about God they do not experience any inner confirmation that the information makes sense.

When I first heard that about the Elohim-God I felt liberated. The Elohim are one level of the nine levels of spiritual beings, described as the Spiritual Hierarchy by Dionysius the Areopagite that put the highest God's intentions into action. These nine levels of spiritual beings were described by Dionysius the Areopagite (to be explored later on), and using his list we can find them identified throughout the Bible, specifically when the words, power, authority, might, principalities, among others, are used.

The Greek word for *Elohim* is *Exousia* and is rightly translated as power – the power to create. Furthermore, the word Elohim is plural and feminine. I have come to understand why this is. They are the creators of form, like a pregnant woman creates the form of her child, and we see their work in every form on this earth. This is like seeing the finished house from the architects plan.

It is clear that no one can explain God to us; we must remove the blindfold ourselves and intelligently discover not just one God but all the Gods who uphold this Universe and keep it in order.

Where is God?

When we are called to praise and worship God, where exactly is God at the time? And, is it important to know where God is for our praise and worship to have effect?

When we enter into the activity of praise and worship there is a sense of raising ourselves up, and therefore we usually look up. Do we think God is up there somewhere?

Often we enter into this activity when things are not going so well. Sometimes it seems that prayer is a way of escaping from ourselves when we defer to a higher being outside ourselves. It takes the pressure off, but we should ask if this deals with the cause of the pressure.

We don't have to look very far to see that we live in a society where people thrive on placing things outside themselves. If we trip on a step and break our leg the first thing we do is look for the fault in the step, it is much more difficult to accept that we were not paying attention to where we placed our foot. Each time we experience misfortune our instinct is to place blame elsewhere. Doesn't worshipping God fall into this same category? Certainly in the face of misfortune, many people question the presence of God.

What if God is actually within us? Paul seems to think so.

"For we are the temple of the living God; as God said, "I will live in them and move in them, and I will be their God, and they shall be my

people." 2 Corinthians 6:16

Paul is the one who opposed Christ Jesus until he had a firsthand experience of the presence of Christ, which caused him to fall to the ground and become blind -we could say that he fell off his under-**stand**-ing and he could no longer look outside himself. This is how it is recorded in the Bible.

"But Saul, still breathing threats and murder against the disciples of the Lord, went to the high priest and asked him for letters to the synagogues at Damascus, so that if he found any belonging to the Way, men or women, he might bring them bound to Jerusalem. Now as he journeyed he approached Damascus, and suddenly a light from heaven flashed about him. And he fell to the ground and heard a voice saying to him, "Saul, Saul, why do you persecute me?" And he said, "Who are you, Lord?" And he said, "I am Jesus, whom you are persecuting; but rise and enter the city, and you will be told what you are to do." The men who were traveling with him stood speechless, hearing the voice but seeing no one." Acts 9:1-7

Through this experience, Paul became aware that each human being can be the temple of the living God! This is what he is explaining in 2 Corinthians. What does *"For we are the temple of the living God;"* really mean in terms of everyday life? *Naos*, the Greek word for temple, refers to the inner shrine or sanctuary of the temple, the Holy Place and the Holy of Holies. A more accurate translation would be, "We are a holy place of a living God."

Then we can ask, what is a living God? The word 'living' is *zao*, has a connection to the resurrection. It was the resurrected Christ that Paul experienced. He spoke of this in Colossians *"the glory of this mystery, which is Christ in you, the hope of glory."* Col 1:27 The living God could be Christ and Christ is IN us, we are his temple. So, instead of placing our issues at the feet of an external God perhaps we should be dealing with our issues within us to make our temple, our inner shrine, the perfect dwelling place for Christ, the living God. This was explored in the previous essay.

Christ in You, The Hope of Glory

Let's look more closely at this text *"Christ in you, the hope of glory"* When Easter has passed, the eggs are eaten and the holidays are over, where does that leave us in relation to the crucifixion? We can't say that Christ Jesus is dead and buried because that is definitely not the case. Jesus' body was never found, only the cloths he was wrapped in. Christ didn't have a body, he wasn't a physical being; he was a cosmic being experiencing physical life in the body of Jesus.

To put a finer point on it, the Cosmic Christ entered into Jesus' blood which then flowed into the earth when the soldier stuck him in the side with his lance. Imagine how powerful that blood was. It contained a Cosmic force from the creative center of the Universe that had never been able to enter into this earth before – just as we couldn't go Mars or Venus unless a vehicle was specially prepared.

The first time the Cosmic Christ was able to exist here was when a vehicle was prepared for it, and that vehicle was Jesus. These are such great mysteries our earthly minds could not possibly understand them fully. So the blood has flowed into the earth – what now? St Paul has an answer.

"....to make the word of God fully known, the mystery hidden for ages and generations but now made manifest to his saints. To them God chose to make known how great among the Gentiles are the riches of the glory of this mystery, which is Christ in you, the hope of glory." Colossians 1:25-27

Saints, *hagios*, are those who have entered into a holy love for the mysteries. Gentiles, *ethnos*, really means the people generally as opposed the select few.

The key words of the mystery are "Christ in you, the hope of glory". *Os Estin Christos en sý ho elpís ho dóxa.* Hope is a confident expectation. *Doxa* refers to the transforming radiance in our being when we form the right opinions, *dokeo*, about the mystery.

So how does this relate to the blood that has flowed into the earth? Everything we eat is grown in this earth. So everything we eat is infused with the powerful blood of Christ. When Jesus was crucified and the flood flowed into the earth Christ was able to assume this earth as his body. Surely this will transform our body, make us look younger, enlivened. So why doesn't everyone look younger and enlivened – including the earth itself? Only those who have entered into a holy love for the mysteries will have this experience. They won't need to tell us that they have had the experience it will be obvious in their transforming radiance.

What is God's Creation?

For most people, the idea of creation begins with the story of Adam and Eve.

When reading the first chapter of Genesis it is good to ask questions. Perhaps not so much to get answers, but rather, to open ourselves to different ideas. God's creation is described in Genesis, which begins with:

"In the beginning God created the heavens and the earth." Genesis 1:1

We delved into the meaning of this text in "Who or What is God?"

Towards the end of chapter 1, after the outer world was 'created', we come to the first mention of human beings.

"So God created man in his own image, in the image of God he created him; male and female he created them." Genesis 1:27

We should take this text literally, *"male and female he created them."* In other words, in the beginning human beings were male AND female, not male OR female. In other words, these human beings were hermaphrodites. Human beings didn't become male or female until the rib story in Chapter 2.

"So the Lord God caused a deep sleep to fall upon the man, and while he slept took one of his ribs and closed up its place with flesh; and

the rib which the Lord God had taken from the man he made into a woman and brought her to the man." Genesis 2:21-22

The big question to ask now is this. Did life as we know it start in the Garden of Eden? Is this the beginning and end of God's creation? At the same time, we should also ask: when Eve spoke to the snake and surrendered to temptation was that really the downfall of the human race. See Genesis 3

The main problem with understanding what actually took place is that we think that human beings were the same then as they are now. How could that possibly be! For a start, who can talk to snakes now? Seriously, we need to understand the true evolution of the human being in body, soul, and spirit. See the beginning of this book which addresses the difference between Soul and Spirit. Paul gives us many clues in Corinthians 15. Let's take a closer look at verses 44 to 46.

"If there is a natural body, there is also a spiritual body. Thus it is written, "The first man Adam became a living being"; the last Adam became a life-giving spirit. But it is not the spiritual which is first but the natural, and then the spiritual." 1 Corinthians 15:44-46

In the Greek it actually says, if there is body *soma* and soul *psuche,* there is also spirit *pneuma.* The word natural is not there. Then it says that the first man, *protos anthropos,* became a living soul, *zao psuche.* This describes a soul that is alive and breathing and we could take it to mean that the first Adam was able to exist for the first time in the atmosphere of this physical earth as soul-being with a physical body that breathes. Paul tells us that this is a crucial step in the process, the first step.

The last Adam, which is a reference to Christ crucified, became spiritually alive, *pneuma zoopoioun.* So this story tells us in detail about the evolutionary process of human beings pointing out that God's creation evolves. If we are to fully understand ourselves as members of the human race, we need knowledge about how these three areas: body, soul, and spirit, function. There is an ongoing process in which we can, in fact must, participate.

At this stage in our evolution we are very aware of our body, our senses are alive, and we spend a lot of time seeking physical pleasure – from food, from contact with others, by keeping comfortable and warm etc. We have a dim awareness of our soul, as if in a dream, and we are mostly unaware of our spirit. Until we can wake up our soul and become consciously aware of its functioning, we will never be able to experience the life-giving spirit of which Paul speaks. It took me 25 years of study and six years of writing to put this information into a format that we can work with in our daily life – you will find it in my book "I Connecting".

If we ever wonder what is wrong in the world today it is that these guiding principles are virtually unknown. Once we start to work with these three areas of our being, we have greater control of the way we respond to life bringing us to the experience of true freedom. This is why John reports Jesus' words in John 8:32 *"you will know the truth, and the truth will make you free."* (See full quote John 8:30-32) Another road to freedom is to become aware of the principles the disciples represent in our being. (See essay coming up, "Why Twelve Disciples?") Then we will understand the ways in which God's Creation evolves.

7 REINCARNATION

Reincarnation in the Bible

Many people find interpretations of Bible texts alienating. They seem to say that we should do this and not do that, for example, have faith and don't sin. This usually indicates a superficial interpretation has been made about the meaning of the text.

More than ever, we need to crack the code and get deep into the Bible to see how it is relevant for our modern lives. Otherwise, the Bible is just a relic.

The Bible is certainly not a tool for moralizing but rather it is a tool for personal development. Nor is it a means to fantasize about a God we know very little about. We will never achieve lasting personal development based on a skewed interpretation of sin and faith. If we unlock the true meaning of the words in the Bible, we will develop our capacity to think things through to the truth of the matter. The trouble is, we often find thinking painful, feeling is much more comfortable. Test this out by reading aloud the next sentence.

The single most important piece of information missing from our daily lives is an understanding of reincarnation.

There are texts in Bible that make much more sense if we apply the principle of repeated earthly lives. I know that many people find the concept of repeated lives on earth difficult to understand. However, we have reached a point in our development where we can begin to remember snippets of our past lives. These are the déjà vu moments. Déjà vu, according to Wikipedia, is a French phrase meaning, "already seen", and it refers to the experience of believing that one has witnessed or experienced a situation previously.

Karma

Here is a brief explanation of reincarnation for those unfamiliar with the basic concept. Our actions in previous lives cause consequences in future lives – we can call this karma For example, if we stole from others in a previous life, people may steal from us in this life, not just possessions but stolen time, stolen effort, stolen ideas etc.. If we looked down on others in a past life, in this life we might be short so that people physically look down on us. If we didn't take in what we heard in a past life, now we may be deaf. Isaac Newton's third law of physics, "For every action there is an equal and opposite reaction" echoes the ancient mystery teaching about reincarnation.

We can bounce to and fro with actions and reactions or we can embrace our experiences and be in harmony with them.

One place in the Bible that speaks of reincarnation is in the eighth Beatitude.

"Blessed are those who are persecuted because of righteousness, for theirs is the kingdom of heaven." Matthew 5:10

This is not speaking about being a martyr, as we shall see when we look at the meaning of the Greek words. The word for 'those who are persecuted', is *dediogmenoi* in Greek, and indicates the ones who are driven away. Who do we drive away from us? The ones with whom we have difficult karma, the ones who cause us to react.

If we think about reincarnation in terms of the history of the human race then we can assume that we have incarnated many times, so many in fact that most of the people we meet have a karmic connection to us. This karma needs balancing which is not always easy. This makes sense if we think about the way friends can fall out and marriages can break down.

If we place the word *dediogmenoi*, driving away, in the context of righteousness a very different story emerges. Righteousness is *dikaiosune*, which means justice or being just, balanced and in harmony. The scales of justice give us a good understanding of the meaning of righteousness. Justice is a continual series of adjustments to restore balance and harmony. This also means that we have the ability to judge when things are 'just right'.

If we want to understand our own past lives we need to look for clues. One big clue is this: notice how we are attracted to some people, and repelled by others. There are so many clues in even the smallest events in our lives.

Another clue can be found in facial expressions. Some people have an uncanny resemblance to people who lived long ago. Obviously only the faces of famous people have survived, and not all of us were famous people in past lives, but the similarity can be uncanny.

When the singer Prince died recently my friend Adriana Koulias discovered that his facial features were a very close match to those of the Egyptian Pharaoh Akhenaten who died around 1335 BC. She then looked into the lives of these two men and discovered many similarities - many actions and reactions. Prince and Akhenaten: Tales of Karma and

Initiation.
Available https://www.amazon.com/dp/B01G34FSY4

If we act on these ideas instead of reacting, we can make a great deal of sense of world events as well as events in our own lives. This brings us peace and harmony, and a deep respect for the wisdom of the Universe - "for theirs is the kingdom of heaven."

Do We Really Understand Destiny?

Every event in our life has deep meaning. Whether an event creates joy or sadness, it is significant. The significance is not fully understood while we have no understanding of reincarnation and karma which can even include those who accept the fact of reincarnation. It is not enough to accept reincarnation and karma as a fact; we need a working understanding of it to give our life its full meaning.

Rudolf Steiner wrote essays for the magazine Lucifer Gnosis in the early 1900s in which he tried to explain spiritual principles as they applied to our daily life. In one article, "How Karma Works" he sets out the idea of "the evolution of the eternal human spirit through many lives." He compares this with the days of our lives saying what we did yesterday affects what we will do today, and so on. We act differently tomorrow according to our experiences today, we have the opportunity to rectify our mistakes and to be better people. In this way, our past is always present with us, always creating the future. In this way we create our destiny.

Activity That has Become Destiny is Karma.

The way we respond to our destiny is the key. "The fact that our destiny, our karma, meets us in the form of absolute necessity is no obstacle to our freedom. For when we act we approach this destiny with the measure of independence we have achieved. It is not destiny that acts, but it is we who act in accordance with the laws of this destiny."

If we apply these ideas to reincarnation we can consider another statement from Rudolf Steiner, "We cannot understand the human individual from ancestors [...] (each of us) exist for a long time before the copulation of our parents. A kind of unaware love leads the child to these certain parents and causes them to begetting."

If we understand that we are in control of our destiny, that we create all the circumstances in our lives from a higher perspective, even to the point of causing our parents to give birth to us, we will view life quite differently. This is an urgent task today as we deal with escalating levels of fear driven by world events.

Reincarnation Means our Parents Don't Shape us, we Shape Them

I came to the understanding that because we reincarnate, we are not a product of our parents. Our parents don't shape us, we shape them. When parents welcome a child they are saying, "Welcome, I am willing to change to accommodate you and I promise to walk with you through the next 21 years to prepare you to become the individual you are destined to become." This would certainly explain why some parents who have difficulty with their child, place the blame on the child by saying, "I have a difficult child." This is the parent unwilling to change.

How often do we look at a tiny baby and think about the man or woman they were in a previous life? Mostly we focus on the biological facts, the parents had sex, the sperm penetrated the ovum, and therefore the parents created the child. Why do we think that this is the source, origin, and cause of a human being? This is only the source of the physical body. The origin lies with the (re)incarnating spirit and the cause has a deep connection with the Logos, the creative Word that lies at the foundation of the Universe.

What we don't realize is that the incarnating child chooses its parents. The choice is based on past-life connections, but also because other people with whom there is a strong connection are incarnating in a similar region of the world. In this way, we give ourselves the greatest opportunity for growth as we deal with our karma and (perhaps more importantly) help others deal with theirs.

By focusing on the incarnating soul, we place things in their right perspective. In this way we can make much more sense of stillbirths, cot deaths and other childhood illnesses. The incarnating soul may only have needed to be in this world for a short period before continuing its preparation in the spiritual worlds for its next incarnation.

If we are able to think these ideas through we go a long way to understanding the purpose of life and our own life's purpose.

The New Commandment, a Prerequisite for Remembering Past Lives.

Why don't we remember past lives? Well, some people do, but most of us don't - consciously at least. The reason is simple; we don't love enough. Not just any love, but a special kind of love which Jesus spoke of when he said, "love one another as I have loved you."

Not being able to remember our past lives means that we don't understand reincarnation and therefore we don't see it mentioned in the Bible. The main reason we don't understand reincarnation is because we lack awareness of our spiritual vision. Our vision is confined to what we can physically see and touch. Yet within the physical lies spirit, spirit gives the physical two things; form and life. When we die spirit leaves our physical form and all that is left is an empty, lifeless shell.

One way to understand this is to contemplate the life cycle of a butterfly; compare the pupa to our body and the butterfly to our spirit.

To come to a firm understanding of spirit, and the

spiritual worlds, we need to continually build our understanding of spirit as an invisible force within us and around us responsible for giving us life and form. It is not something "out there."

Love

When we begin to traverse the boundaries of what we can see and touch, we realize that one of the most spiritual things we do in life is to love. Love is not something "out there" either it is an activity we constantly experience in one form or another. We can't touch love, but we can see it in the expression on people's faces and in their gestures and deeds. Through love spirit reaches out to touch us.

Love is a complex and even mysterious feeling. It has many layers and different expressions. We can even disguise our hatred as love. In the Bible, we see how love plays out in the life of the man Jesus as he took into himself the Cosmic Christ. Even though he was berated, mocked, scorned, and immobilized on a cross, he never stopped loving.

Jesus is the role model for our own journey of spiritual growth; we can apply his experiences to our inner self, within our consciousness. Our inner Jesus is that part of us that always tries to act in a higher way, that part of us yearning for purity, purity necessary before the Christ impulse becomes an active part of our consciousness. This is not a straightforward process as we soon discover.

As we begin to commit to a higher expression, something within us then mocks and immobilizes us. We hear an inner voice saying, "Don't be such a goody-two-shoes, you could be bullied for that." In this way we are mocking, scorning, and crucifying our inner Jesus.

This leaves us asking the question: how was it possible for Jesus to love so much that he could bear all that he bore on his journey to the cross? The answer tells us how we can recognize the presence of Christ in this world, in us and in each other.

The New Commandment is the answer:

"This is my commandment, that you love one another as I have loved you." John 15:12

Love is not a simple straightforward feeling; it has various expressions. The Greeks used at least four different words for love.

1.   *Eros* is erotic physical love. Eros is the Greek god of fertility. This is passionate love involving sensual desire and longing. This kind of love leads to procreative urges to ensure the survival of the species.

2.   *Philia* is the love arising in friendship and even in business connections. There is mutual admiration that can be supportive and nurturing but also exclusive. If the usefulness of the relationship changes, so can the relationship.

3.   *Storge* is the love of family, tribe and nation. It can be defensive and aggressive to those outside the group. This is the kind of love we also find in the animal kingdom.

4.   *Agape* is the highest love. We can call it divine love, Christ-ened love. This love is expressed by those who experience the highest in themselves - which they also see in others. It speaks of unification and intense compassion. This love is expressed without fear or favor and therefore it is not sentimental. It may not always be interpreted as love because it can cut like a sword.

In the New Commandment the word used for 'love' is agape, "that you agape-love one another as I have agape-loved you." This is the only love strong enough to enable us to see our own past lives. Why? Because seeing our past lives requires agape-love to be able to deal with the consequences of our actions in a past life - our karma

Generally, we respond to our karma by blaming the other person for what they have said or done to us. Instead, if someone undermines us, we need to look for the cause in our own actions in a past life - perhaps we caused them to fall through a floor, or lose their footing somehow.

Facing our karma takes courage and it takes agape-love for self. Paul knew this which is why he wanted to record these words for perpetuity.

"Do not be deceived; God is not mocked, for whatever a man sows, that he will also reap." Galatians 6:7

There are many quotes in the Bible about reincarnation, and many references to agape-love. When we truly understand the purpose of living repeated lives on this earth, we come to understand that karma is a blessing; it enables us to act in a higher way. It also enables us to experience agape-love. The higher our response to our karma, the closer we come to a true experience of Christ Jesus.

8 THE DISCIPLES

Why Twelve Disciples?

The Bible clearly states that there were many more disciples than 12. Luke gives one example of this.

After this the Lord appointed seventy-two others and sent them two by two ahead of him to every town and place where he was about to go. Luke 10:1

In the Bible we find two different words to describe these close companions of Christ Jesus, disciple and apostle. In Luke 10, the word 'sent' is *apostello* or apostle. Is there a difference between a disciple and an apostle? If we look at the ancient meaning of these two words, we see that they are two different aspects of the same person.

The Greek word *apostello* comes from *apo* which means 'of separation'; and *stello*, meaning to set in order or arrange. It speaks of getting ready for something new, preparing for something separate from the way it used to be. In addition, the word *stello* comes from *histemi* which means to cause or make to stand. The thing that causes every human being to stand on two feet is the I Am, setting us apart from animals. This could mean that the apostle is the one who now stands on his or her own two feet.

Disciple in Greek is *mathetes*, which means more than the basic interpretation of 'thoughtful learner'; it means the learner who uses the principles of mathematics to understand the truth. This may sound weird but if we think about it, it makes sense. It refers to using the principles of mathematics to test the truth, to ensure things always add up. There is a special word for this which has been used in secret societies down the ages which is *mathesis* - and we can see the word 'maths' in these two words. Therefore, we can say the *mathetes mathesis* - which means disciples understanding truth. This, of course, is a continual process of testing and re-testing as we do in mathematics to ensure things always add up.

This brings us to the question: why does the Bible focus on 12 disciples, and why does it mention that there were more than 12?

I would like to suggest that the disciples represent certain human characteristics, I have written about this previously in my book "I AM The Soul's Heartbeat Volume 4, The Twelve Disciples in the Gospel of John". The meaning of their names explains their nature and in this way shows us different aspects of our own character which we need to develop. The disciple in us, *mathetes*, is the one who learns, and the way we learn is through thinking accompanied by endeavor. Most thinking today is not accompanied by endeavor. In fact, many people are very lazy with their thinking, which is why they never fully understand this world – or themselves.

Not only do the 12 disciples represent 12 different characteristics, they also represent 12 ways to understand or approach spiritual truth. This could mean that one person approaches spiritual truth in the Andrew way, while another approaches it in the Phillip way. It is said that there are 12 paths up the mountain.

Let's take a look at the basic nature of the 12 disciples who followed Jesus. We can observe these qualities in ourselves throughout the day to see how they work in our consciousness. We can also identify our own approach to truth.

Disciples Andrew, Simon Peter and Phillip

Andrew: In the Gospel of John references to Andrew reveal that he works in the background; he is a companion. Andrew represents strength of mind and humility; therefore, these two faculties must always be our companions working away in the background. Andrew is from Bethsaida, a fishing town. Fish represent our thoughts, our ideas, our concepts, and so Andrew comes from a place where ideas and concepts are caught.

Simon Peter: Simon means hearing and Peter means faith. Simon Peter captures the essence of our ability to hear and see beyond the physical sounds and images that meet our senses. The Simon nature becomes active when we deeply contemplate something and a new understanding seems to speak from within us like an inner voice. This is the true nature of inspiration; we hear the new idea with our inner ear. The Peter nature means that our faith becomes knowing, rather than blind faith. We are able to confirm our inspirations again and again in our contemplations. Here we can see *mathesis* at work.

Phillip: The name Philip means lover of horses just as the word philosopher means lover of wisdom. Philip speaks to us about inner power, courage, and an ability to weigh things up. Philip is the challenge within us to use our mind purely intellectually or to allow a spiritual element to enter in that doesn't rely so much on physical proof, but can certainly be tested over and over again in our thinking.

The use of the term spiritual does not mean something airy-fairy. By spiritual is meant something that can't be physically touched, for example, love is spiritual, a hug or kiss is physical. This points to a notion that behind everything physically present in this world there is something spiritual, just as love sits behind a hug or a kiss. If we look for the spiritual component behind all that is physical in our lives a whole new world opens up to us.

The disciple in us develops in an intimate way before being expressed in the world as the apostle - the one sent. This is not evangelical, converting others. Why do some people focus on converting others when the whole idea is to focus on converting ourselves? When we do this with success others witness what we have done as an example of what is possible for them.

By working out the unique ways in which we tread our own path, we can be more accepting of the ways in which others tread theirs.

Disciples John, Thaddaeus and Matthew

The road from disciple to apostle has one purpose; to open us up to the experience of our Higher Self referred to in the Bible as *ego eimi*, I Am. If we speak these two words, "I Am" out aloud and imagine standing in the Universe, beyond the idea of time and space, we get a sense of this eternal state of being. Yesterday, today and tomorrow open up to us as one place. In this way, we claim our own individuality without the weight of opinions and the ideas of society. Try it, it is refreshing. When we come back to the present our outlook has changed. It is from this perspective that we can view the disciples.

We can imagine their incredible journey with Jesus - the one who experienced his I Am first - and stand in their shoes as they approach their own I Am from their unique perspective. This was not without trepidation as we read in the Bible.

We can ask what it was like for John, Thaddaeus, or Matthew when they journeyed through the Middle East with Jesus as he challenged the status quo. Each one experienced it through the qualities given to them by their name.

As previously suggested, while the disciples represent qualities in our mind or consciousness, they also represent the different paths that we each take as we strive to connect to the highest, purest human condition, our I Am. At this stage in the evolution of consciousness, we are about halfway there. As with all things, some are a little ahead, some are a little behind. This does not mean we can pass judgment on others, it simply means we each take a different path.

John: The name John means 'the grace of the Lord' and he represents love and grace. This love is *agape*, one of four main Greek words for love, discussed above. Agape as the highest love, loves everyone equally; it does not favor family over friends and acquaintances, nor does it favor one's own culture over another.

In its highest expression, love is objective. It does not see through the eyes of judgment, but understands human behavior as a developmental process we all go through. This love is not biased and it does not take offence. It is a kind and understanding witness, always recognizing the pure human seed within each human being. Then, seamlessly this love fertilizes the seed in the other person opening it to its inner potential. From this comes the expression of grace.

Grace is that capacity in our soul for doing what is right, what is good, out of our inner self, not through externally imposed rules and regulations. Grace says, "How can I be so that you can be free." *Charis* is the Greek word for grace - which reveals the word charismatic. This is when love shines from us in an inspiring way. Other people want to become like us and they do this of their own accord, not because we give them advice about how they should be.

Thaddaeus: Thaddaeus represents elimination, letting go of things so that we can keep moving forward. The name Thaddaeus means 'of the heart', big-hearted, warm-hearted. The disciple Thaddaeus is also known as St Jude and was a brother of St James the Less, and also a relative of Jesus. It is the heart which can eliminate things that mesmerize the mind. Thaddaeus within us works continuously to restore harmony by eliminating that which disrupts. This is tied to forgiveness.

Forgiveness is not so much about covering up what we feel, but by stepping over it and moving on. To assist this, we could work with John and adopt love and grace.

Matthew: Matthew represents our will - our intentions and actions. Matthew collected taxes. He works in the depths of the community to sustain the body - the infrastructure - of society. He was called away from that to serve in the innermost circle so that human will could become freewill. The other thing about will is that it reveals ourselves to us. Our acts of will, when, for example, we dig the garden or rearrange the furniture, give us a glimpse of ourselves, of our ability and place in the world.

We can take these as separate paths, or working in conjunction with one of the other disciple-paths, and find our way to our Higher Self. Using the disciples to become more aware of our character and qualities, and the particular path we are on, is the ancient recipe for personal development untainted by modern trends that often accentuate self-importance. This is the ego trying to displace the I Am - feeling threatened by it actually. By accepting our own path, and remaining open to the path of others, the whole human race will climb the mountain with more certainty and security.

Disciples Nathanael Bartholomew, Judas and Thomas

Why did Jesus have disciples? Couldn't he go it alone?

Asking such questions can lead us to different perspectives regarding our own spiritual journey. If we are totally honest with ourselves, all we want is to understand ourselves. Then, the next thing we want is to understand others. Looking into the lives of the disciples can assist with this.

When we look at the disciples the first thing we notice is that each disciple is different, yet they walk together, and they walk with a leading principle called Jesus. This does not mean that we should look for a leader outside ourselves, but rather look for a leading principle within us.

When we look at the characteristics of the disciples we will identify with one more than another. This can reveal to us the path we are on, and another disciple can reveal the path a friend is on, this should not be cause for disagreement. Yet this is often the case; it is a common principle today that unless you agree with someone you are against them. This has a stifling effect because unless you have the strength to support your own ideas you are silenced in one way or another.

Apart from describing our different paths, each disciple represents mind traits. We can think like Thomas in one situation, and respond like Judas in another. Understanding the twelve traits revealed in the nature of the disciples, we can understand ourselves better, and find ways of responding to life differently. Also, if we can identify where other people are coming from - a Judas or a Thomas trait - we will meet their ideas with understanding and life will be more harmonious.

The next three disciples show that the conventional interpretation of them is actually the opposite of what they really represent as mind qualities. This is often the case when we investigate beneath the surface to discover spiritual meanings.

Nathanael Bartholomew: Nathanael means gift of God. He is known by his family name, Bartholomew, in the Gospels of Matthew, Mark, and Luke. John calls him

Nathanael. In my book on the Disciples "I Am the Soul's Heartbeat - The Twelve-Disciples" I show how Nathanael is the faculty of imagination within us. Not fantasy but real imagination - a spiritual imagination able to create concepts as living images. By creating moving pictures in our mind when we try to understand a concept brings it to life. Also, these concepts will be much easier to remember. This is a method used by people who have excellent memories, and inventors also think this way as they work out the detail of their invention.

What this means is that we 'see' things differently. Jesus points out to Nathanael that this is only the beginning: *"You shall see greater things than these."* This must always be our expectation, to see greater things. We should always strive to have firsthand experiences, by hearing Philip within us saying, "Come and see."

Judas: Judas represents the generative, reproductive energy within us which can work in a positive or negative way. Judas is said to be the Greek version of the Hebrew name Judah which means 'praise Jehovah'.

"And she conceived again and bore a son, and said, 'This time I will praise the Lord'; therefore she called his name Judah; then she ceased bearing." Genesis 29:35

The reproductive force within us is motivated by conservation, survival of the species. Judas is also associated with betrayal, however, the word 'betray' also means to 'reveal'. Judas gives us the opportunity to act in a higher way.

In my book on the Disciples I speak about him in this way. "There are two sides to the Judas energy within us. He can assist us or assail us. Mostly he works within us without our knowing. It is up to us to become conscious of what he is doing. Jesus was."

Thomas: Thomas represents reasoning, understanding. Thomas' central role in some of the Bible stories alerts us to the imperative of reasoning. He doesn't take things at face value, he wants to understand and experience things fully. His questioning can be described as a lack of faith or disbelief, however, blind faith is like a blind person crossing a busy road alone.

The Thomas in us continually tests the facts from every side to reach a full understanding. Generally people do not do this; they stop at the first understanding that satisfies them, which is usually only a fraction of the truth. This is lazy because we take the easy way out so that we have instant answers without much effort. What is not realized is that the effort we put in awakens our consciousness. We don't need to find the ultimate truth, or have it given to us by others; it is the striving we need.

Disciples James Alphaeus, James Zebedee and Simon the Cananaean

When we think of Jesus and his Disciples, we should be equally mindful of the mighty Cosmic Spirit called Christ gradually becoming infused into the body of Jesus. Only when we think of this being in this way can we approach the truth of the situation. There were two beings, Jesus the man and Christ the Being who had never experience life in a human body before. Imagine that! This happened for the first time in the whole Universe. Think about what it is like to do something for the first time; learning to swim, learning to drive, learning to ski, taking your first roller coaster ride or first bungee jump. Magnify that thousands of times and we may get some idea.

The other side of this story is that humanity cannot move forward without Christ. That is why he went through the process of entering into the man Jesus. We cannot evolve without Christ - not that he does the work for us, no, quite the opposite, we do the work which he has made possible, and he enhances it.

"Truly, truly, I say to you, he who believes in me will also do the works that I do; and greater works than these will he do, because I go to the Father." John 14:12

For Jesus to go through the mighty transformation of taking into himself this mighty Cosmic Being required the support of the disciples, just as we need support when we learn to swim, drive or ski. Stop and think for a minute what it would be like to be infused by a being of the stature of Christ. Luke knew when he wrote about the Son of man - the Christ infused human:

"For as the lightning flashes and lights up the sky from one side to the other, so will the Son of man be in his day." Luke 17:24

Are we ready to be struck by lightning? For that is what it is like when Christ becomes active in our being. For that lightning to be effective, we have to make some choices. Otherwise it will burn us or kill us. To survive the strike, the 12 mind faculties represented by the disciples have to be activated in a positive way.

It is a work in progress and we should go easy on ourselves. We can be so critical of ourselves it can be crippling. It is about building pictures for ourselves and taking baby steps. The last three disciples speak strongly about choice. Having choice is so free making. We should always be mindful that if we can make a choice in one direction then we can also make it in another.

James Alphaeus: James the son of Alphaeus represents order, especially creating order in chaos. He is also known as James the Less, or James the Just and is a half-brother of Jesus. James is connected with the use of the word; speech is a very creative thing, primarily because it gives us choice. We can choose to speak or not to speak, and we can choose what to say or what not to say. We can also release a power in what we say, as Jesus did when he said, *"Laz'arus, come out"* for instance. James is associated with the power in us to say something, perhaps something difficult. James is also the discipline in us not to say something. Our speech will be orderly according to how conscious we are.

James Zebedee: James the son of Zeb'edee represents the faculty of judgment or discrimination within us. Judgment is that higher ability not be swayed by our self-will, or the will of others. It also helps us to resist being drawn back to the past and to stand in the present, in the new situation, and seek to express our higher will. Within us, our intentions are our will; without, will is visible in our actions.

Simon the Cananaean: Also known as Simon the Zealot who probably belonged to the Zelotes, an extreme Jewish sect. This sect was also known as the Cananaeans. Simon was the brother of James and Jude. After the martyrdom of James, Simon became head of the Church at Jerusalem. In hermetic tradition, the zelator is the one who is able to approach the fire. Simon the Cananaean stands for zeal, enthusiasm; this motivating energy is optimism for the future.

9 SPIRITUAL BEINGS

Discovering Spiritual Beings

There is so much to consider when trying to unlock the Bible. Firstly, there are many concepts that are not part of modern understanding. In a science driven society we are told that if we can't touch it, it's not real. However, more people probably accept rather than disagree that Angels are real. Unless we open our mind to possibilities we will never understand the vast unseen world that surrounds us and maintains physical life.

Close examination of some of the words in the Bible reveal that there are many unseen spiritual beings at work in the heavens and in the earth. To gain some understanding of this we can look back to the work of Dionysius the Areopagite, the anonymous theologian and philosopher of the late 5th to early 6th century.* He described these beings in his work called The Celestial Hierarchy http://www.tertullian.org/ The Austrian philosopher, Rudolf

Steiner, also described the functions of these beings very clearly.

This is what I wrote several years ago at the beginning of my detailed study of The Revelation, the last book in the Bible.

"Before we continue we should take a moment to consider the many spiritual beings mentioned in these first six verses of this Revelation of Jesus Christ to John. Our modern intellect has difficulty straddling the concept of beings that are not visible. Although, consider that for some people, God, Jesus Christ and the Devil are perfectly acceptable spiritual beings, and, for some others, Angels exist. For the most part we don't really have adequate images of the different spiritual beings or powers that are an integral and essential part of life in the Universe. As we travel through this Revelation we will meet many of these beings and come to understand something of their role in our existence." Kristina Kaine

Ed Smith, in his wonderful reference book, "The Burning Bush" lists them. He explains them in this way,

"Between (the) Trinity and Humanity were the Hierarchies ... The Hierarchies are ninefold, being in three ranks of three. The highest rank comprises, in descending order, and using their names as reflected in scripture, the Seraphim, Cherubim and Thrones; the second rank (though variously ordered by different Christian authorities) comprises the Dominions, Powers and Authorities; and the third rank the Principalities, Archangels and Angels. (Rudolf) Steiner gave each of these a name in keeping with its character in the creative process. The Greek terminology corresponded with the English terms, but it is noteworthy that the Hebrew term for "Authorities," or for the "Exousiai" in Greek, was "Elohim," the plural term used for God in Gen 1."

It is these Elohim that John refers to in The Revelation when he says "and from the seven spirits who are before his throne". See my essay above about the Elohim in "Who or what is God?"

119

Many of the spiritual beings in the Bible are broadly considered to be God. However, understanding that God can have different expressions gives us a much clearer picture of the spiritual company we keep. Then we start to see how we are affected by the actions and functions of these beings that we could say stand above us (as we stand above plants and animals) yet exist in our environment - but we could also say that these beings are in a different dimension. Furthermore, we could say that these beings have a greater or different experience of the Universe than we do.

We should not take lightly the different ways these beings are referred to, for in their names we find clues to their roles e.g. dominions, powers, and authorities.

I will now try to explain the functions of the different beings and show why they are mentioned in the Bible and how that relates to our life today.

* Regarding Dionysius the Areopagite, Karl Konig in his lectures published in The Grail and the Development of Conscience, says that Dionysius "was not the name of an individual but of a holy office." He also points out that the central figures in Raphael's painting, The School of Athens, are St Paul and Dionysius not Plato and Aristotle which most people assume.

Are Angels Real?

In 2009 the results of a survey about what people believe in was published in an Australian Newspaper http://www.theage.com.au/national/god-is-still-tops-but-angels-rate-well-20091218-l5v9.html. In this survey (which of course is never representative) it says, "51 per cent of respondents say they believe in angels". I would like to ask those 501 people what exactly they think Angels are.

The Greek word *angelos* means messenger. We know that a messenger takes a message from one place or person to another and the purpose of a message is to inform.

Therefore, we must ask several questions.

o   What is the source of the message that the Angel receives?

o   In what form of communication can a message be conveyed to us?

It would be over-simplifying the situation to say that the Angel carries a message from God. Earlier we explored the notion that there are different 'gods' or spiritual beings who have certain responsibilities in the Universe to keep everything in balance. Dionysius the Areopagite listed them, and soon we will explore them further.

Angels feature often in the Bible, for example, in this quote bringing a message about the birth of Jesus.

"But as he considered this, behold, an angel of the Lord appeared to him in a dream, saying, 'Joseph, son of David, do not fear to take Mary your wife, for that which is conceived in her is of the Holy Spirit;'" Matthew 1:20

One reason for this communication between Joseph and the Angel is the fact that Angels are the closest spiritual beings to man. They are the interface between the physical and spiritual worlds. Angels are beings who are one stage higher than human beings, as animals are beings one stage lower than humans. As we care for our animals, so Angels watch over us. Archangels like Gabriel and Michael are one stage higher than Angels, putting them two stages higher than humans.

We could say that Angels are like human beings without a body. This assists us to understand these beings but we should also know that when we no longer need a physical body we will be greater beings than the present Angels. This is because we are in a different evolutionary stream. The difference between Angels and human beings is that human beings have the I Am, the element which makes us unique. Paul tells us about our relationship to Angels in Hebrews:

"Thou didst make him for a little while lower than the Angels, thou hast crowned him with glory and honor," Hebrews 2:7

The present task of the Angels is to be intermediaries who help and guide the evolution of human consciousness. We could even say that they are interpreters of what higher spiritual beings want to convey to us; what these higher beings 'say' is then made intelligible through the Angels. Of course, they wouldn't use language; they speak to us in images – the universal language. For example, the image of a tree means the same thing to every human being on earth.

While some people might doubt the validity of these ideas, I could point out that animals communicate with each other, and with us, in ways we do not fully understand. Communication is an important topic for human beings at present. We live in unsettling times where fake news is a thing. We could ask ourselves if we are willing to believe fake news without any fact checking, why can't we also believe in Angels?

If we can remain open to ideas about the presence of Angels and other spiritual beings not visible to our physical senses, we will be surprised by the new insights we will have. We will come to know that we each have a Guardian Angel watching over us. The messages we can receive from the Angels can give us an inner sense or feeling that confirms something is true. Not that we should just believe anything, the ideas we receive should be continually tested. In this way, we can be lifted out of the present darkness that our mind cannot penetrate. For each of us this is a personal experience, we do not need to convince others of it; we can only hope that others come to their own experience of the Angelic beings in this Universe.

The Spiritual Hierarchy

Angels, Archangels and Archai

For decades I have thoughtfully studied the Spiritual Hierarchy, these nine levels of beings upon which the regulation of this Universe depends. From the transience of a breath of wind, every movement of clouds, to the dependable movement of planets and stars, all these are purposefully guided by beings beyond our imagination.

Whenever I contemplate this hint of knowledge I try to see its place in my life otherwise such knowledge is empty theory. What place do Angels or Archangels have in our lives? Naturally, these beings are complex and since we hardly understand the makeup of our own being, how can we expect to know theirs. Not to be defeated we should have confidence to start somewhere.

What we can know is that all efforts to understand, and even experience, the work of the Angelic beings connect us with them in some small way, which in turn assists them to experience the human condition. Even though these beings guide and regulate the Universe for our benefit, they have a different consciousness to ours. Just as we don't understand them, they also do not understand us. It is as if we are in separate rooms and the thickness of the walls depends on the level of our own conscious awareness. The more we connect to our I Am, the more we can connect up with these beings and see them at work in the Universe.

This Spiritual Hierarchy is best viewed as three teams of three: Angel, Archangels and Archai; Powers, Mights and Dominions; and right at the top Thrones, Cherubim and Seraphim. Above them is the Trinity – Father, Son and Holy Spirit.

Angels

So let's look at the group closest to human beings; Angels,

Archangels and Archai. Put simply; Angels guide people, Archangels guide nations and Archai regulate human evolution.

We could say that while we remain unaware of our I Am, our Guardian Angel acts on its behalf leading and guiding us through life. As we connect up with our I Am our Angel can stand back a bit. What a comforting notion to think that we are held and guided by an Angelic being in all that we do. If we have any prayer life at all it should be directed to this being who lovingly embraces all that we do, even our shortfalls. This lovely prayer gives us a sense of the support we receive from our Guardian Angel.

Prayer to the Angel
You, my heavenly friend, my Angel,
You who have led me to the earth
and will lead me through the gate of death
into the spiritual home of the human soul;
You, who have known the path for thousands of years;
Never cease to enlighten me, to strengthen me, to advise me,
that I may emerge from the consuming fire of destiny
a stronger vessel
and learn ever more to fill myself
with a sense for the goals of the spiritual world.
Ernst Karl Plachner 1896-1982

Archangels

The Archangels are a step higher than Angels. When a person has a great influence on a nation, either by leading it or by influencing it, we could say that they are connected to an Archangel. They have their Archangelic being within them assisting them to do their work. Whenever a new leader of a nation is elected I have always watched them very closely to see how the Archangel of the nation changes them, and when they step down you can see that the Archangel has left them. Of course, it isn't the same Archangel for every leader.

The Bible only uses the term Archangel twice, in 1 Thessalonians 4:16 and Jude 1:9, in other places just the names of the Archangels closely connected to the evolution of mankind are mentioned; Michael, Gabriel, Raphael or Uriel. In Daniel 12:1 we read, *"At that time shall arise Michael, the great prince who has charge of your people."* Note that his passage points to the task of the Archangels when it says "charge of your people."

There are various orders of Archangels and each has a leader. Michael is the leader of all the Archangels, Gabriel who cares for mothers preparing to give birth, and Raphael the guardian of healers.

Archai

The Archai lead mankind as a whole and their work is influenced by the numbers of human beings who increase their spiritual awareness. When we do not work on become more spiritually aware we weigh down these beings. We find reference to these beings in the Greek word *arche* or beginning. This word is sometimes rendered 'principalities' or 'rule' and indicates their work on human consciousness. When changes in the consciousness of humanity occur, it can indicate a change in the activity of the Archai.

These ideas give us a sense of movement and change. The more conscious some of us become the greater the activity of these beings which in turn affects us all.

Powers, Mights and Dominions

The next three members of the Spiritual Hierarchy are the least known but they appear many times in the Bible. We could refer to these nine groups of beings that comprise the Spiritual Hierarchy as grades in the angelic orders. As part of a Hierarchy, we could also say that they do what is required of them according to the beings above them, who in turn receive their direction from the Trinity. You can read the original description of these beings by Dionysius the

Areopagite
http://www.esoteric.msu.edu/VolumeII/CelestialHierarchy.
html

I sometimes imagine them as a pyramid of champagne glasses and the champagne cascades from the top to the bottom filling all the glasses. In the case of the Angelic orders, each glass would have different properties because each of the orders has its own particular realm of operation. They would also relay the prevailing conditions below them up through the Hierarchy to those above so that all are informed. This function becomes even more important as human beings express their freewill; these beings have the task of rebalancing unconscious human actions which affect the Universe - there is much to be considered about this.

This middle trio of the Spiritual Hierarchy works more in Creation as a whole using wisdom (dominions), to set things in motion (mights), and create form (powers or *exousia*). We find a fine example of their place in the scheme of things in Colossians.

He is the image of the invisible God, the first-born of all creation; for in him all things were created, in heaven and on earth, visible and invisible, whether thrones (Greek thronos who are part of the top trio), or dominions (Greek kyriotetes or principalities) arche – (part of the bottom trio) or authorities exousia --all things were created through him and for him. Colossians 1:15-16

N.B. It will not be accidental that in this text *thronos* are placed next to *kyriotetes* and *archai* are placed next to *exousia*, for that is how they are connected in the angelic orders.

Powers

The first of these three, the ones closest to the Archai, are the Powers or *Exousia*. *Exousia* signifies freedom of action, the right to act, and they are what I call the creator gods who work with the element of fire or heat. They are the ones mentioned in Genesis 1. The Hebrew term for the Greek *exousia* is *elohim* translated as God in Genesis 1:1 considered earlier. This term is also plural which supports the notion of members of an angelic order. They are the Spirits of Form working through heat to create the physical substance of this earth. See "Who or what is God?" for more on this.

Mights

Mights, *dunamis,* can be found to be translated as power in Bible which confuses their role with the *Exousia*, the creator gods. They are associated with the element of air, and have their domain in motion and therefore work in the wind and movement of the clouds among other things. The clue to the way they work in motion is found in the way their name relates to dynamite. There are many translations for the Greek word *dunamis*; ability, abundance, deed, meaning, might, miracle, strength, violence, virtue and work.

Dominions

Dominions, *kuriotetes*, essentially means lordships (*kurios* means Lord) and indicates authority. They are associated with the element of water. Here is an example of how they are mentioned in the Bible in Paul's letter to the Ephesians.

...according to the working of his great might which he accomplished in Christ when he raised him from the dead and made him sit at his right hand in the heavenly places, far above all rule (arche) and authority (exousia) and power (dunamis) and dominion (kuriotetos). Excerpt from Ephesians 1:15-23

We could say that the Mights give motion to the form created by the Powers under the lordship or wisdom of the Dominions. In this way our Universe is regulated – but with orders from above according to the prevailing conditions below in human beings, nations, and the needs of evolution.

Here is an example of the work of these beings, "The teachings of Christ spoke not only to the understanding of the listeners, but led living forces from the spiritual world into the souls of the people. This is indicated in the gospels with the words: 'For he spoke with the power of authority, and not as one of the scribes.' Matthew 7:29 "The Cycle of the Year" by Hans-Werner Schroeder

The words 'power' and 'authority' indicate the involvement of members of the Spiritual Hierarchy which bring the spoken word, the Logos, to us. Powers or *Exousia,* as discussed, are the 4th level of the Hierarchy. *Exousia* signifies freedom of action, the right to act, and they are the creator gods who work with the element of fire or heat. Authority is referring to Dominions or *kuriotetes,* which essentially means lordships (*kurios* means Lord) and indicates authority. They are the 6th level.

As Hans-Werner says, these are "the living forces Christ led into the souls of the people."

Thrones, Cherubim and Seraphim

While the first hierarchical group is concerned with human consciousness, and the second is concerned with the outer environmental patterns of the Universe, the third and highest group, who look into the face of God, the three in one, is concerned with the highest spiritual values of creative will, harmony, and love.

The Trinity pours out their ideas into the order of Seraphim who then share these with the Cherubim who then figure out what the ideas mean, and then the Thrones transform them into action. It is this action of the Thrones that we experience as creation. Yet it isn't the Thrones who do the creating, they pass on the creative impulses to the Spirits of Form, the creator gods referred to in the Bible as *Elohim* or *Exousia.*

It is very helpful to see how these different angelic orders work in concert. Even this highest group of beings, who look into the face of God, are so removed from us we can experience them through the Angelic orders closest to us; the

Angels, Archangels and Archai.

Since the work of these orders is all about the development of human consciousness – and it is awesome to think of all these beings focus their efforts on human life – it should be the least we can do to try and have ideas about their work.

Love, Harmony and Will

So how can we form some relevant ideas about love, harmony and will and make them part of our own lives? It doesn't help to form these ideas from the modern usage of these words because these beings are the highest and purest of all the Angelic orders. We could say that they hold the archetype of Love, the plan of what love should really be in its purest form, the same for harmony and will. However, we do find these three things in our everyday lives, they are the faculties of our soul; feeling, thinking and intention. Love is the highest feeling; harmony is the combining of ideas, which is thinking which enables judging; and will the highest creative action.

At present these three faculties work mostly unconsciously in our soul. If we are to become consciously aware then this is where we start. As soon as we become conscious of the feelings that course through our soul, and as we are able to guide them in different directions, we begin to touch on the work of the Seraphim, the Spirits of Love. When we become aware of the thoughts that occupy our mind continually, and we can concentrate enough to change them into more constructive and productive thoughts, then we connect up with the work of the Spirits of Harmony, the Cherubim. When we are able to direct our intentions most creatively with the purest motives, and become consciously aware of the power of our own will, then we begin to understand the work of the Thrones, the Spirits of Will.

Hopefully these short notes on this mighty Spiritual

Hierarchy will be food for thought. We can find them mentioned throughout the Bible and if we apply the things that they represent to the story in which they are mentioned we will unlock a deeper meaning to this sacred book. The common refrains, "Praise God", "Praise Jesus," or "Praise the Lord," are just empty distractions from our everyday life. Don't leave your troubles at the door and get high on praising an unknown God. Get to know the gods and the work they do, you will be rewarded. Instead of standing outside the door of a house and saying, "Praise the house", we can enter the house and give thanks for all the individual effort that makes a home clean, orderly, safe, and nurturing.

For a more detailed look at the Disciples see "I AM The Soul's Heartbeat: The Twelve Disciples in the Gospel of St John" available on Amazon

10 BIBLICAL PRINCIPALS IN LIFE

Spiritual Understanding Cannot be a Pretense

It often amazes me when I explore the original meaning of the words that are used in a Bible text. On the surface we can easily say that we understand what the words are relaying to us. But when we look at the original words, words that the translators obviously didn't fully understand, (nor could they interfere with them thank goodness), we find quite a different story.

If we always keep in mind that we are spiritual beings using a physical body to live on this earth for a while and apply that understanding to a text like Matthew 6:16-18 a new story emerges. If we fast it means that we stop the physical world entering into us, this relates to our physical body, but it also relates to the limited ideas of this world. Anointing, *aleipho*, speaks of the sacred placing of oil on a person who has died, or a person who will now devote themselves to spiritual work, as a priest does. Our head is that place where the life forces, the etheric forces are concentrated. These forces are plant-like and plants go through a cycle of seed to flower then death, which creates the new seed. To wash, *nipto*, which means cleanse, the face is pointing to cleansing our astral body, which is the expression of our emotions and feelings. These activities are ongoing in those who have committed to experiencing their spiritual being.

"And when you fast, do not look dismal, like the hypocrites, for they disfigure their faces that their fasting may be seen by men. Truly, I say to you, they have received their reward. But when you fast, anoint your head and wash your face, that your fasting may not be seen by men but by your Father who is in secret; and your Father who sees in secret will reward you. Matthew 6:16-18

This is saying that we cannot put on an act. When we abstain from eating don't pretend and look sullen, hiding our real motives. This is egotistical. Those who pretend will have their reward, *misthos*, get what is due to them. When we fast, anoint and wash, cleansing our physical, etheric and astral bodies, do it not to be seen by others but for inner transformation, which will be rewarded *apodidomi,* which means to discharge what is due, to restore.

We have such a sense of inner privacy that we think that we can feel, think and will whatever we like. It is our business. We happily think things that we would never say. This is pretense, this is being hypocritical. Perhaps we enjoy the feeling of freedom that comes with thinking whatever we like, but that is not what freedom is. Freedom comes when we can stop ourselves from thinking things that we would never say to a person. Freedom comes when we can stop ourselves from feeling hurt or disappointed. This freedom comes when we experience life through our I Am, which is our spiritual being. The other freedom is bound to our astral and its instinctive egotistical responses.

When we experience true freedom through the presence of our I Am in our soul this inner experience is rewarded, *apodidomi,* our karma is discharged and we are restored.

What Does it Really Mean to Repent?

Having looked at the some of the most important principles in the Bible, we can now look at some of the terms which are not often understood, and often misused.

"Repent," "turn," "stop sinning," "ask God for forgiveness," is the clarion call from pulpits all over the world. Is it clear what we should actually do? This preaching comes from these Bible texts:

"From that time Jesus began to preach, saying, 'Repent, for the kingdom of heaven is at hand.'" Matthew 4:17

"but unless you repent you will all likewise perish." Luke 13:3

What are we to make of this today? What does it actually mean to repent? Don't we need to know what it means if we are to do it? In fact, we could even ask what it means to be good, i.e. not sin. We can only find some real answers to these questions if we first consider human consciousness, and assess how consciously aware our mind is.

Changing Consciousness

We also need to consider the ways in which human awareness changes over time; the way we use our mind evolves and our consciousness becomes increasingly individualized. If we accept this, it means we are thinking for ourselves much more than we ever did, just as a child does as it matures. Unless we understand the way in which our consciousness - our mind and awareness - changes we can't begin to fully understand the Bible, especially words like repent and sin.

Observing the way our consciousness changes as we age is a good way of grasping the idea of changing human consciousness. We also know that we think differently from our grandparents and even our parents. Apart from this difference between generations, there is another important way to look at changes in consciousness. If human consciousness changes over thousands of years, couldn't we compare this with the way it changes in one human being during their lifetime. For example, we could say that if primitive man thought like a 10 year old, then at present, by comparison, we now think like a 35 year old.

If this were the case, it would mean that when the New Testament was written people's thought processes were less mature than ours are today. This might lead us to question, as many people do, the relevance of the Bible for us today. The question that arose for me personally was whether the Bible was written for a certain kind of consciousness or whether it can be applied across time and still be relevant - particularly when I came across words like repent and sin, among others.

I have been writing about my understanding of the Bible since 2003 and have studied it since 1983, which has enabled me to see the Bible as a map of developing human consciousness. I have found many examples of this over the years as I examined the original Greek meaning of words, and it amazes me how pertinent these ideas are for us in the 21st Century as we move from local to global interactions. I see how our expanding awareness means that we have to think differently on many levels. At the same time, many people seem to live their lives unconsciously even though they now have the opportunity to be more conscious than ever before. It is time for all of us to wake up!

How do we Repent?

What does this have to do with repenting? Just as we re-engineer the workplace to accommodate the changing ways we do business, so we must also re-engineer our mind. As Einstein famously said, "We can't solve problems by using the same kind of thinking we used when we created them." Furthermore, when we begin to understand how our consciousness can change, that in itself changes it! It is as if we put a magnifying glass to our own thoughts, feelings, and actions.

We also know that the pace of change is quickening. Just as technology always needs updating, so do our patterns of thinking and ways of living. I can see that the human race has reached a point of intensity in its development. In this condition of intensity we are asked to repent. It happened two thousand years ago, and it is happening now. Change could even be perpetual.

So, what does it mean to repent? This word means something quite different from the way we use it today. It isn't about being sorry or regretful, and it certainly isn't about asking for forgiveness; it could be about changing our mind, but how?

In the Greek language, the word repent is *metanoia* which literally means 'to perceive afterwards'. It implies that we can see the consequences of our actions before we act. We could call it foresight although it is more than that. It is about placing ourselves in the future and consciously experiencing firsthand the effects of, not only our actions, but also our thoughts, and feelings.

Repent means to be very observant, acutely aware. This level of awareness applies to our speech, our emotions, and our intentions. It means that we accept a new level of responsibility. Each day the news reveals how many people do not consider the consequences of their actions before they act. They feel free to express themselves without concern for the effects of their words and emotions on others.

To see 'in real time' the affect we have on the future changes everything about us. This is what it means to repent.

What is it to Sin?

Sin is one of the most misunderstood concepts today. All too often it is tied to guilt and fear which has the potential to be psychologically disturbing. "If you don't do A then B will happen to you." Surely this will not discourage us to avoid sin, but rather motivate us to conceal sin.

In the New Testament, the Greek word for sin is *hamartia*, which literally means 'to miss the mark'. Think of an archer pulling on the bowstring to point the arrow at the target. Think of the archer's body; every muscle aligned with precision, eyes focused on the target, coordinated breathing, stillness, and full concentration. To hit the target the first time, and every time after that, is expecting a lot.

Let's take a look at the word 'sin' in this Bible text.

"Receive the Holy Spirit. If you forgive the sins of any, they are forgiven; if you retain the sins of any, they are retained." John 20:22f

Let's begin by examining the words, *"if you forgive the sins of any."* The Greek word for 'any,' is *tis;* it is an interrogative pronoun used in order to ask a question: who, which, what? It doesn't necessarily refer to others; it can refer to us by applying it in this way: 'If you forgive the sins of yourself, they are forgiven;'

Forgive is *aphiemi* made up of two words; *apo* and *eimi*. *Apo* means separating the part from the whole, or distancing ourselves; *eimi* means 'to be', as we might say, "I just am." Forgive therefore, suggests a state of harmony and balance, and a position of recognition (although not necessarily acceptance).

Then there is the matter of retaining sins. The word 'retained' is *krateo* which means to have power, to be powerful. Whenever we want power, we usually have the wrong motive. We enter into a state of compensation rather than just being with whatever is happening.

Understanding the meaning behind the Greek words shows us that sin is a state of non-perfection, which has the possibility of becoming perfection. Then sin becomes something constructive, part of our goal. With this attitude, we have the courage to keep pulling on the bowstring, working on our aim and our poise.

When we have developed a certain level of skill we are able to see how we have underperformed. When it comes to sin, this takes courage. Usually we are inclined to make excuses for missing the mark; it was someone else's fault. Then we engage in the power of retaining sin, rather than the recognition required for forgiving sin.

The Role of Love

If we are going to hit the mark, we need to work out what the mark is. What target, as human beings, are we aiming for? Surely is it love, the New Commandment: *Love one another as I have loved you.* John 13:34

This love understands; it has the right perspective. It is a love that recognizes the effort involved in honing the archer's aim. We become objective and in this way, we stand in the other person's shoes and see, not their failure, but how, step by step, they sharpen their aim. We also apply these same principles to ourselves.

We could also say that we sin when we don't make an effort to understand sin. Without this understanding, we perpetuate sin. Our task is to aim the bow by recognizing the right way from the wrong way. No-one else can do this for us, not any law of government or religion, but only our own understanding of who we are as human beings and where we stand in the Universe. There is an ancient saying, "Man, know yourself!" and as we work towards knowing ourselves we become much more aware of our motives. The true meaning of sin gives us the courage to objectively recognize how we miss the mark and work on perfecting our aim.

When is the Judge the Killer?

When we think about the nature of God, it is good to consider the word judgment which is so often linked with him. The image of the man with the beard sitting on a throne watching and judging everything we do is a bizarre concept. It suggests that God is a giant sticky beak!

Take, for example, these words from the Gospel of Matthew which records Jesus saying:

"You have heard that it was said to the men of old, 'You shall not kill; and whoever kills shall be liable to judgment.' Matthew 5:21

Let's ask what is being killed and who is judging? Sure, in the next verse Matthew's report continues about being angry with your brother but the logic of my ideas about verse 21 applies also to the subsequent verses when we identify the brother as something within us.

The specific Greek word used here for 'kill' is *phoneuo* which means to murder. Murder means to kill secretly when no one is aware of what we are doing. What happens within us secretly that no one is aware of? The forming of our opinions! All day long we decide what is good and bad mostly without being fully informed. Therefore, in our consciousness, with our thoughts, feelings and intentions, we secretly take the life from people and things that displease us. What is more, we think it is our right to do this while at the same time demanding that someone who physically kills another person is punished with a jail sentence or a death sentence.

So who is the judge? The judge is actually the killer. Judgment in Greek is *krisis* and means separating (analyzing) and then a decision. Yet how often do we separate out all the facts? Modern life is full of quick decisions. If we want to stop being the killer, the one who takes the life out of something, we must take the time to do the separating.

This Greek word *krisis* is similar to the English word crisis that means a critical moment or a turning point. In daily life it is our opportunity to be aware of all the facts before we make damaging statements, or act prematurely. This means we need to be much more aware of all the issues so that we stop, separate out all the facts, and put them back together differently before making decisions - then the judge is no longer the killer.

Soon Afterwards he Went to a Town Called Nain

A closer look at the Greek words used in the bible, even in simple statements, can reveal surprising new meanings. Take, for example, a simple statement like this,

"Soon afterwards he went to a town called Nain," Luke 7:11

In the Greek it says: *And egeneto, en ho echn poreuomai eis polis kaleo Nain*

Egeneto means that something came into existence, something was born. *Echn* doesn't mean 'day' it means 'what happened next'. *Poreuomai* indicates a procedure or an experience and can mean 'to go to the other side'. The side that we are on mostly is this physical world, we are not aware of the other side of the physical which is the spiritual world. *Poreuomai* can indicate an awareness or experience of the spirit behind matter.

Kaleo does not mean 'named' it speaks of a calling, an inner impulse to a particular course of action. For example, it can indicate to be called to a certain task.

So what is being said here is not about a group of people walking into a town; it is saying that their consciousness changed. A new awareness was born within them because of an inner calling. So they experienced a different consciousness which was connected with Nain, which means beauty.

Our experience of beauty occurs in the life-force of our body, our etheric body. The etheric life-force is found in nature, and in us it is the force that keeps us alive. When this force leaves us we die and when we look at a dead body we see that it has gone. To become aware of this life-force look deeply at a beautiful flower and notice how you feel as you fully take in its beauty. You might feel a lightness, a swelling, a glow. This feeling could remind you of the growth-force of a plant. If you stay focused on the flower you might then have some new ideas about the perfection of the creative force that creates such beauty. You might not be able to put it into words but you will have a sense of silent knowing. This is the experience that Luke is describing in these few words. Read the rest of Chapter 7 to place these words in context. They speak of a widow whose son has died.

When Should Women be Subordinate?

When someone knocked on my door wanting to explain the Bible to me, I told him that I was already a student of the Bible, at which point he enthusiastically suggested that he come in to compare notes. As I was thinking about how he would not enjoy that, he quoted Paul to me. I responded saying, "Paul didn't like women." He looked shocked and quietly left. I wonder if he has been studying 1 Corinthians ever since to try and work out why Paul speaks about women the way he does.

Take this verse for example:

"the women should keep silence in the churches. For they are not permitted to speak, but should be subordinate, as even the law says. If there is anything they desire to know, let them ask their husbands at home." 1 Corinthians 14:34,35

How can such a doctrine stand today when the importance of gender equality is broadly recognized? A closer look at the actual Greek words used by Paul reveals quite a different meaning, especially if we apply them to what goes on within our consciousness. After all, it is within our consciousness that we recognize gender equality.

The Greek word translated as church is *ekklesia* from *ekkletos* meaning called, from *ekkalein* to call out, from *kalein* to call. In what circumstances do we call out? We can call out for help, we can call out to get someone's attention, or we can make a call to challenge in some way. Behind the word 'call' is the activity of bringing attention or awareness to something.

What are we called to become aware of? Primarily, we are

called to become aware of the activity in our soul: our feelings, thoughts, and intentions. So many thoughts, feelings, and intentions are active in our consciousness in a robotic, impulsive way. It can be quite a shock to become aware of them. When we call them out (ekklesia) we gather or assemble them in a focused way. This sounds like a church doesn't it?

Now we must ask: what are the wife and the husband within us? In a very basic, generalized way we know that the feminine nature is the nurturer, filled with feeling. The male nature is more practical, more pragmatic, based on thinking. Our task is to encourage these two to work together so that feeling warms the coldness of our thinking and thinking guides our feeling to be practical.

With these ideas in mind, a new picture of what Paul is saying emerges. When Paul used the word 'subordinate', which in Greek is *hupotasso* where *hupo* means under, and *tasso* means to arrange, we can understand that he is saying we arrange our feelings under our thoughts and in this way we keep our emotions under control.

Then Paul says,

"If there is anything they (women) desire to know, let them ask their husbands at home."

Continuing on with the idea that Paul is speaking about the activity in our consciousness; we can ask questions of our thinking in the privacy of our own home, i.e. our inner being. This should always be the case, to question our thinking, which in turn makes us aware of our thoughts. This is when we can discover how often they are negative, fueled by our emotions. With this awareness, we can keep them silent, *"not permitting them to speak."*

What does this say about knocking on people's doors with our own ideas about what the Bible means! Unlocking the Bible is now up to each individual person. Asking the husband-thoughts within us to assist us to make sense of sacred texts, and not letting our wife-feelings run away from us, is important work for every human being.

We Commit Adultery Everyday

"You have heard that it was said, 'You shall not commit adultery.' But I say to you that every one who looks at a woman lustfully has already committed adultery with her in his heart. Matthew 5:27,28

If we apply some basic logic to this text, we can only conclude that it makes no sense to our modern minds. Is it all about sex and lust or is it pointing to another harmful activity? Firstly, there is no mention of a particular gender lusting after women here, it says every 'one' pas, meaning each one individually. This leads us to ask if the word 'woman' means something else.

Gune, woman, points to a stage in human evolution as described in Genesis. The human spirit, Adam, took on a soul, Eve. For the first time in human evolution, every one, individually, took on this soul form. In its most elemental state, it is our innate feeling nature. As we work to humanize this part of our nature we raise these feelings up above a certain instinctive level. This happens as we start to see our place in the world. We can imagine Adam and Eve looking around them and seeing the garden, and the animals and birds and it would have given them a different sense of themselves as being separate from the garden and the animals. We know from Genesis that this sense of self, with the help of the serpent, led them to an experience of shame. That is another story.

If we stick with the idea of this new soul-awareness that came with the 'woman' we can imagine that we would be lustful for all that we saw in the garden. Lustful, *epithumeo*, means to be passionate. In this sense, the soul can be consumed by passion. *Epi* refers to position -on, at, by, before and *thumeo* actually means a very agitated anger. The purpose of anger is to give us the opportunity to conquer it.

If we think about that for a moment we can experience the level of force within us that is required firstly to allow the anger to rise up, and then, secondly, to contain it. If we reach a level of expertise with this process, we will then experience our spiritual Imaginative ability where living images give us spiritual insight.

So what then is an adulterer? *Moichos*, an adulterer, metaphorically means one who is faithless toward God, so they have lost sight of the God with whom they dwelt as spiritual beings. In other words, there has been a breach in the relationship between the soul and the spirit. The soul is more attracted to worldly things and at its lowest level is not interested to do the work necessary to achieve, of its own accord, the mastery required to individually and personally experience spiritual insight.

It is interesting that this should be experienced "In the heart". Our heart is a most mysterious organ, grossly misunderstood by science. When our emotional life matures to the required extent, we actually start to think with our heart (and feel with our mind). This relationship between feeling and thinking lies at the core of what is said here in this text. If we continue to feel with our heart and think with our mind we commit adultery.

Staying Calm in the Face of Fear and Anxiety

Things will get more intense while human beings fail to experience soul and spirit – in themselves and in the world. However we do this is up to us, but do it we must.

When we regard ourselves simply as physical beings, and this earth as dust, we are essentially committing the soul and spirit to suicide. We can do this in the smallest ways during the day when we give our body priority over our soul and spirit.

For instance, when we eat, do we think of all the forces of man and nature that made it possible for the food to be on our plate? Or, are we grateful to all those who deal with our waste?

Not being mindful of these things closes us off to the soul and spirit of the earth and leaves us with feelings of fear and anxiety. The only resolution is to know that our spirit is eternal and the only way it can be damaged is if we ignore it. How do we ignore it? By not developing our soul faculties of thinking, feeling, and will through which we can remain calm and relaxed in the face of any event.

"Whatever the next hour or day may bring, I cannot change it by fear or anxiety, for it is not yet known. I will therefore wait for it with complete inward restfulness, perfect tranquility of mind. Anyone who can meet the future in this calm, relaxed way, without impairing his active strength and energy, will be able to develop the powers of his soul freely and intensively. It is as if hindrance after hindrance falls away, as the soul comes to be more and more pervaded by this feeling of humbleness toward approaching events." Rudolf Steiner Metamorphoses of the Soul Paths of Experience Vol. 2 Lecture 4 Nature of Prayer

My book I Connecting explains in very simple terms how to experience soul and spirit.

"We are at a crisis point in evolution, a pivotal time for humanity.

This book explains that we are beings of body, soul and spirit and that, for too long, knowledge of our soul and spirit has been ignored. Do we have a complete picture of a car by describing its shell, its shape and colour, while ignoring the engine, mechanics and the driver? The truth is that our physical body without our soul and spirit is just an empty shell. There is a good case to make that, because we think of our total being as just a physical body, we are at such a crisis point.

[…]

It is like driving a car down a foggy road; the headlights of the car shine through the mist to illuminate everything. The strength of the light depends on the liveliness of our soul. This image demonstrates how our "I" works through our body and soul, using the faculties of feeling, thinking and willing to the extent that it can connect with our soul. There are moments when the lights shine brightly, the "I" has put them on high beam, and we see more than the fog that surrounds us. We have a wider view, one that places us in relation to the world. The "I" is driving the car (our body) and through the headlights (our soul) it can have a wider view. The reflected light assists us to see within the car as well. Take a moment to create this image in your mind and experience the interaction between your body, soul and "I"." I Connecting by Kristina Kaine

Seeking rest from troubling times

As we try to make sense of what is happening in the world, we can often feel quite defeated. When this happens we find ourselves in need of consolation. There are numerous ways to console ourselves; we can reach out to many distractions and substances. But is this the solution? Or, does this mean we are drawn away from our purpose?

It is easy to be distracted from our purpose when we are not clear about our purpose. As I continually say, our purpose is to consciously experience our I Am, our Higher Self, in our soul. It lies there dormant until we do.

We can only really come near it when we have the courage to know that when saying "I", which makes us feel important, this sense of "I" is only a mirrored reflection of our I Am. Experiencing the truth of this can be very troubling. We need ways of centering ourselves - of finding our I Am center.

One thing that works for me is to repeat these words to myself.

"Come to me, all who labor and are heavy laden, and I will give you rest. Take my yoke upon you, and learn from me; for I am gentle and lowly in heart, and you will find rest for your souls. For my yoke is easy, and my burden is light." Matthew 11:28-30

There is something about these words that is at the same time powerful but also mystifying. I thought I would explore the meaning of the original Greek words to see if I could reveal their true meaning. This, of course, is not fully possible, but at least a few hints can assist us to use these words to calm and center ourselves and help make sense of these changing times.

The I Am is Near

The words, "Come to me" in Greek are *deute pros ego*. It is no surprise to find hidden within these words 'ego eimi', which mean I Am. "Deute" is an imperative form (no room for questions) of *eimi*. A new translation of "Come to me" can be "I Am near".

When the I Am is near we can certainly feel weary and overloaded by the change that must take place in our soul. Weary, *kopiao* and heavy laden, *phortizo* refer to what happens when we focus on the physical and ignore our soul and spirit, we become exhausted and weighed down. "I will give you rest" where 'I' is not *ego* but *kago* which means the 'self-same' that is, the I Am. Rest is *anapauo* which means to keep quiet, to be of calm and patient expectation. This is exactly how we should approach the inclusion of our I Am in daily life.

We can say:

"I Am near all who labor and are heavy laden, the same I Am will give you rest."

Furthermore, we have to do it. We cannot beg for assistance from something outside us. Only when we show that we can do it ourselves will be assisted - assistance which we do not need to request. Our work makes evident that we are ready for assistance. Then our prayers are of gratitude for the assistance we receive.

The Yoke

Let's now have a look at the words, *"Take my yoke upon you, and learn from me; for I am gentle and lowly in heart, and you will find rest for your souls."*

Take, *airo* means to elevate, to raise up. So we step up and elevate all that we are and take the yoke. The idea of a yoke suggests submission but when we look at the Greek meaning, it is more suggestive of equality. The word 'yoke' is *zygos* from the root of *zeugnumi* (to join, especially by a yoke) but it also means a balance, a pair of scales. This means that we raise ourselves up as balanced people who feel equal, who give dignity to the human being.

When we raise ourselves up and we balance ourselves, than we can learn from the I Am. Learn is *manthano* which means to learn by use, to put into practice, not just learn with the mind.

"for I am gentle and lowly in heart". I am, *ego eimi*, the I Am, is gentle. It might seem frightening at first but it is gentle; this is the gentleness of spirit, it is the meekness that arises in us when we connect with our I Am. Lowly is *tapeinos*, an ancient Greek word of uncertain derivation, which we take to mean low or poor. Being meek and poor points us to the Beatitudes. Blessed are the poor in spirit, blessed are the meek. One aspect of this is our ability to recognize and accept that we are meek (lowly) and poor, and we feel this in our heart, which is the center of all physical and spiritual life, and is not weak but strong. Then we are not tempted to puff ourselves up with egotism.

"and you will find rest for your souls." Find, *heurisko*, means to discover within ourselves a way to rest *anapausis* which means a cessation of labor. It is like finding peace within our souls. Soul is *psyche*, the seat of feeling, thinking and willing. When we bring peace about in our soul, and we have to do it by quietening all the activity which undermines us, we will also find great strength.

"For my yoke is easy, and my burden is light." So when discover the equilibrium that comes with the yoke we also see that it is easy, *chrestos*, fit for use and manageable. In other words, we can handle it. The burden, *phortion*, something we bear, becomes bearable, it is light *elaphros*, light in weight, it

quickens us and gives us agility.

We shouldn't kid ourselves about the I Am, it is daunting, but if we can find the courage within us to work with it we will be elevated and strengthened beyond our expectations. Believing this is the best way to start. Recognizing how weary it makes us feel, how weighed down, is a sign that we are on our way to personally break through the barriers that separate us from our spiritual self, our I Am.

Peace - are we Doing it all Wrong?

Peace is such a popular word, we use it frequently as a Christmas greeting, we use it daily when stressed, and we use it in response to war.

The strangest thing about peace is that there is always an expectation that it will come from an external source, "I send you Peace and Joy," or "Give me some peace!" or "We want peace!", or "Let us declare peace!" This kind of peace comes with a price: the price of compromise and protracted negotiations. It usually calls for a peace treaty, not only between governments but also in personal relationships - a contract that imposes conditions of agreement.

When we really understand what peace is, we realize that this view of peace is superficial. To deepen our understanding of peace we can explore its meaning in the Bible where we find terms like Prince of Peace or Lord of Peace. Why is Christ Jesus referred to as the Prince of Peace or the Lord of Peace? His path to the cross on Golgotha was less than peaceful. Only when we ask the questions, "Is peace given to us?" or "Is it up to us to find this peace?" can we begin to discover the true meaning of peace.

Eirene is the Greek word for peace and indicates freedom from disturbance, stillness. *Shalom* is the Hebrew equivalent which means soundness. This means that peace means to be still, to be sound, to experience inner harmony. This is a personal experience, not something that comes to us through others. We harmonize all that is discordant within us. Indeed, we can say that the noblest response is for us to be peaceful in the face of adversity, and the lowest response would be to expect someone else to do something so that we experience peace.

Imagine what it would be like if people took up the responsibility to achieve harmony within themselves, to be still, to achieve their own inner peace whenever their peace was disturbed.

I have written about this process before where I suggest that each time our equilibrium is disrupted we place ourselves in the upper room. To achieve this we create the imagination of the disciples meeting in the upper room after the crucifixion, and Christ appears among them. It says that he walked through the wall (because the doors were locked), and the disciples experienced intense fear. To help build a vivid imagination read the story in the Gospel of St John, Chapter 20:19-31. Three times Jesus says, *"Eirene humin,"* "Peace to you" which essentially means remove the disturbance within you and reinstate soundness.

If we try to do this when something fearful happens to us we know how hard it can be. The human condition is one of fear and therefore we need all the help we can get to deal with fear. I suggest that whenever we experience inner disturbances that we create in our minds an image of Jesus standing before us saying, "Peace to you." This reinforces our own ability to reinstate inner harmony. By repeating this practice over time, it will become second nature and be of great assistance whenever we are alarmed. When we do this with success, we know that we have to create peace within ourselves. If we wait for it to approach us from outside we will never experience it.

This is one of the most powerful stories I have ever read about peace and love.

"In May 1945, immediately after the end of World War II, George

Ritchie, a young American soldier, found himself with a group of American physicians in a German concentration camp near Wuppertal. They offered medical assistance to the thousands of former prisoners who were close to dying of starvation. In the midst of this unimaginable misery, Ritchie encountered a man who made a profound impression on him. He stood out among the other prisoners because, in contrast to them, his bearing was bolt upright, his eyes clear, and he had a virtually inexhaustible energy.

Since he spoke five languages fluently, the Americans appointed this man interpreter, in the course of which he was tirelessly busy helping people for 15 to 16 hours a day. He radiated an atmosphere of love and compassion from which others drew nourishment. Ritchie called this man, a Polish Jew, 'Bill Cody'. To Ritchie's astonishment he had apparently spent many years in this camp, during which he lived on the same starvation diet as all other prisoners and slept in the same disease-infested barracks. But unlike the others he did not look like a living skeleton.

Each group in the camp seemed to regard him as their friend. If a quarrel erupted he was called to arbitrate and mediate. He also continually talked with the former prisoners, who were so locked into hatred that they wished to shoot every German on sight, and urged them to forgive their enemies. When Ritchie comments that this will not be easy for them after all they have experienced, Cody tells him his own story, as follows:

We lived in the Warsaw ghetto, my wife and I, our two daughters and our three small sons. When the Germans reached our street they put everyone against the wall and opened fire with their machine-guns. I begged to be allowed to die with my family, but because I spoke German they put me on a forced-labour crew. He pauses for a moment and continues: At that moment I had to decide for myself whether to hate the soldiers who were responsible for this or not. It was in fact not a difficult decision. I was a lawyer. In my practice I had seen all too frequently what hatred can do to people's body and spirit. Hatred had just cost the lives of the six most important people in my life. This is why at that moment I decided that for the rest of my life—whether this was a few days or many years—I would love everyone I came in contact with.

Ritchie suddenly realized that this—love for everyone—is the force that had kept this man, Bill Cody, so healthy and fit despite all the misery and deprivation he experienced." "Time for Transformation - through Darkness to the Light" by Margarete Van Den Brink and Hans Stolp.

When we Pray What do we Hope for?

The Bible is full of secrets; many of them are easy to find if you have the key. As we have discovered, the main key is the Greek language in which the New Testament was written. Although sometimes, we just need to take it literally as in this case.

"But when you pray, go into your room and shut the door and pray to your Father who is in secret; and your Father who sees in secret will reward you. And in praying do not heap up empty phrases as the Gentiles do; for they think that they will be heard for their many words. Do not be like them, for your Father knows what you need before you ask him. Pray then like this: Our Father who art in heaven, Hallowed be thy name. Thy kingdom come. Thy will be done, On earth as it is in heaven. Give us this day our daily bread; And forgive us our debts, As we also have forgiven our debtors; And lead us not into temptation, But deliver us from evil. For if you forgive men their trespasses, your heavenly Father also will forgive you; but if you do not forgive men their trespasses, neither will your Father forgive your trespasses." Matthew 6:6-15

The nature of prayer is misunderstood; many people see it as an opportunity to petition an unseen deity to benefit self or others. This is unnecessary as Matthew reports, *"your Father knows what you need before you ask him."* So if prayer is not for petitioning "our Father" what is it for? We could then say that it is for thanking this deity for benefits bestowed. That may be helpful but does it really tell us about the nature and purpose of prayer?

If we follow the words in this text closely we are told: *"Go into your inner chamber and shut the way into it."* This suggests that we will cease our outer activity and withdraw into ourselves and shut the way into it by stopping all the extraneous thoughts about our daily life. Or, we could continue our daily duties and stop worrying about life knowing that *"our Father"* is on the case. Then our life becomes continuously prayerful.

The word 'prayer' is *proseuchomai*: pros, meaning before or towards, and *euchomai* which means wish or would. A wish is an unfulfilled desire in our soul and the most powerfully unfulfilled desire in our soul is to know who we are and where we came from – our source. This state of being 'before' or pre-fulfillment of the wish, gives a sense of forward movement, of inner striving. Now we come closer to the meaning of prayer. Prayer is about our inner striving to know truth which, if we achieve it, will unite us with spirit; our personal spirit and the spiritual condition of the Cosmos. We could call this an inner communion. If we can achieve it we will be filled with a feeling of gratitude." From "Who is Jesus: What is Christ?" Vol2 by Kristina Kaine

The Last Shall be First

The Bible reveals some amazing secrets about human evolution if the spiritual principles revealed by Rudolf Steiner about the soul and the I Am are applied to the original Greek words.

In the Gospel of Matthew Chapter 20 is a story about a vineyard owner who hires some workers off the street. The vineyard owner went out 5 times during the day to find workers. At the end of the day he paid everyone the same; those who only worked for one hour got the same as those who had worked all day. Naturally they complained. The owner responded in this way.

"But he replied to one of them, 'Friend, I am doing you no wrong; did you not agree with me for a denarius? Take what belongs to you, and go; I choose to give to this last as I give to you. Am I not allowed to do what I choose with what belongs to me? Or do you begrudge my

generosity?' So the last will be first, and the first last."

This is what I wrote about this in the series "Who is Jesus : What is Christ?" Vol 4. The translation of this text, *"Or do you begrudge my generosity?"* is so wrong, and so misleading.

"The householder, the Lord "went out" exelthen which means to appear, make one's appearance, which metaphorically means to come into being, to arise, to come forth. This would suggest movement after a period of rest. The times that the movement took place; early in the morning, then the third, sixth, ninth and eleventh hour, and finishing in the evening suggesting a cycle of time. So the question is: why is each laborer, each lifetime, worth the same amount regardless of the time worked?

To make sense of this we have to try and understand the meaning of the words, "So the last will be first, and the first last." If we think of a plant that grows to maturity, say a tomato plant; the last thing to develop on this plant is the tomato and the tomato is the first thing to die. The plant from which it grew is the first, and it is the last to die when the season is over. If we ask what is the most valuable part of this process we could say that it is the fruit, the "last which will be first". If so, could we say that the tomato is more valuable even though it has only been working for the shortest time? A further thought is that it is only when the plant produces the tomato that we can identify the type of plant, or the breed of tomato. This means that we only fully understand this plant when we look at the last thing, not the first thing.

The Lord's response to the complaints is interesting. The translation is completely wrong, the text does not say "Or do you begrudge my generosity?" It says: is your eye, opthalmos, ponerous - which essentially means: is your eye deceiving you, because the I Am is good? The Greek says, ego agathos eimi, where ego eimi means I Am and agathos means to be good in character and beneficial in effect.

So the first laborer, the aspect of the I Am that agreed to incarnate first has worked for the longest time to support the final fruit - the laborer who was sent into incarnation at the eleventh hour." Kristina Kaine

The Parable of the Lost Sheep

The Bible presents us with so many mysteries that we can hardly know what to make of it. We could study all the ancient principles or we could apply stories like the parables to our lives today. I choose the latter because it seems more relevant, but this is not the only way. What truly amazes me about the Bible is that you can look at it from so many different angles and by painting another view, and another view, eventually see that it is the same picture. Let's take a look at the famous parable of the lost sheep.

"Now the tax collectors and sinners were all drawing near to hear him. And the Pharisees and the scribes murmured, saying, "This man receives sinners and eats with them." So he told them this parable: "What man of you, having a hundred sheep, if he has lost one of them, does not leave the ninety-nine in the wilderness, and go after the one which is lost, until he finds it? And when he has found it, he lays it on his shoulders, rejoicing. And when he comes home, he calls together his friends and his neighbors, saying to them, 'Rejoice with me, for I have found my sheep which was lost.' Just so, I tell you, there will be more joy in heaven over one sinner who repents than over ninety-nine righteous persons who need no repentance." Luke 15:1-7

Here we have two opposing groups of people; team one is the tax collectors and sinners, and team two is the Pharisees and scribes. It would seem that Christ Jesus is saying that the team one is comprised of the lost sheep, and team two is the other ninety nine he doesn't need to worry about – or is he?

Sheep are defenseless and innocent animals; they can represent within us the purity of the human spirit. Christ Jesus is described as *"a sheep led to the slaughter"* Acts 8:32

One way to look at this story is to see how we are all sheep, we have been herded onto this earth and here we huddle in one big flock. Some of us collect taxes, some (most of us actually) sin - *harmatia* - which means to miss the target, some join elite religious (or political) groups and some of us study and write about the laws which guide life. We are all in *eremo*s, the wilderness, alone, disconnected from our spiritual home. Our humanity is lost, *apollumi*, we cannot see who we really are; we have lost that conscious awareness of our place in the Universe. We all think we have the right job, whether we collect taxes or preach religious or political maxims; we are a cozy part of the flock. If we are to restore what is lost we have to leave the flock. We have to die to the flock and be resurrected to the experience of who we really are.

The target that we are aiming for is our 'I' being, our I Am, which is that part of us necessary to becoming fully human; *anthropos* is the word translated as 'man' and it points to the human being who has reached full humanity. This *anthropos* discovers what is lost and when he discovers it – *heurisko* translated as 'find' but speaks of discovery – of course the response is to rejoice, to be glad, *chairo*. It is like a homecoming and we gather our friends, *philo*, those with whom we share a brotherly love because they have also made this discovery, along with our neighbors – those who are nearby and who have an inkling of what we are experiencing, to *sugchairo*, rejoice, with us. This rejoicing is about experiencing others as if we were them. It is a very intimate sharing that belongs to the human I Am which gives us the ability to stand in the reality of each other's experience.

Then verse seven should read: there will be more joy in heaven over one person who changes their mind *metanoia* (repents) about missing the target – the target being to connect up with our I Am – than the ninety nine who **have,** *echo* (this word does not mean need) no repentance; they are those who cannot change their way of thinking.

Destiny and Karma

Article written for the Anthroposophical Prison Outreach in 2017

If you are part of the Anthroposophical Prison Outreach program you will be reading this from a prison cell and in some way a life struggle has gotten you there. Is this fate, is it karma? You no doubt ask: How does this situation belong to me?

Also while in prison you have found Anthroposophy. Again you ask: what can this mean? Can we look at our destiny and come to a deeper understanding and meaning behind the challenges and gifts we face? Can we see that each challenge is an opportunity with a purpose? So you ask: Can I live to a fuller potential while incarcerated… Can I experience deeper spiritual awareness, threshold experiences, in prison?

We cannot begin to answer such questions without understanding that every human being is a work in progress. Each day every human being has the opportunity to become greater than they were yesterday. Yet, moving forward isn't always a continuous motion, sometimes we have to take a few steps backwards to be able to jump a bit higher. It is also true that the higher we climb the more care we must take.

Usually these ideas are applied to the one life we live now and this can leave us with a sense of failure. However, when we consider these ideas in the light of repeated lives on this earth, we can see that a backward step can be in preparation for much larger step forward in some future life. Not that this should become an excuse, but rather a motivation to see more clearly beyond the confines of a restricted view of life.

The biggest question to arise when we consider the possibility of repeated lives is this: Why would we want to live many lives on the earth, especially if this life is so challenging?

We live many lives for several reasons. One reason is to develop qualities for use in later lives, another is to experience what each time-period has to offer, again to be used in later lives. To make sense of this let's have a quick look at what constitutes a human being.

Most people who read Rudolf Steiner's books are aware that human beings are beings of body, soul, and spirit. To put that more correctly, we are beings of soul and spirit and we have a body.

"Do we have a complete picture of a car by describing its shell, its shape and color, while ignoring the engine, mechanics and the driver? The truth is that our physical body without our soul and spirit is just an empty shell." Kristina Kaine

I quote from my book "I Connecting" in which I explore in detail these three elements of every human being. How we function as human beings depends on how conscious we are of these three elements, as well as the way in which they interact with each other.

What I call the 'I-being' is often translated as ego in Rudolf Steiner's work. I prefer to call it the human 'I-being' because the term ego can be confused with our egotistical activity or our lower astral instincts. Here is a more detailed description of the three elements we are made of from my book.

"Our body is the vehicle, our soul is the engine and our 'I' is the driver.

When we say that feeling, thinking and willing are soul faculties, remember that while they originate in the soul they are expressed in the body. It is our body that carries the expression into the world; the soul is the engine and mechanical components, and the 'I' is the driver. The quality of the driving depends on the maturity of our I-connection." Kristina Kaine

To understand how we live repeated lives on this earth we need to acquaint ourselves with the driver of the vehicle. It is the driver who reincarnates, each time in a more up to date vehicle, hopefully the latest model, and who gathers together certain soul expressions according to the karma to be dealt with. These soul expressions amount to the way we feel, think, and behave.

Karma arises when we crash into things. We might not be looking where we are going and this distraction damages our vehicle or someone else's. We always have the opportunity to repair the damage - in this life or the next. Not that we should say, "better luck next time," we must always take full responsibility for the way we drive our vehicle.

Understanding Karma

So what is karma? Karma is a process of weighing and balancing, if we tipped the scales a little too much one way, now we can work out exactly what it will take to bring the scales back into balance. This could be as simple as responding to someone with love and understanding when they back into our car. Or, on the other hand, by getting angry with them we give them the opportunity to feel ashamed for not being more careful - or, so that we can feel ashamed of our own feelings of anger for them, and so on. We can never judge what lies behind each person's karma, as we often don't realize what is behind our own karma.

How does karma arise in each life? When we died last time, we reviewed our life backwards, taking into account everything we did, and then we create a to-do list of what needs to be done to balance out what we did in the past. Eventually we tick everything off and there is nothing more to be done, which signals that it is okay to take our last breath. Or sometimes, we were not able to get through the whole list, so some of the things are carried over to be dealt with in a future life.

The thing about karma is that we need to be conscious of it, most of the time we are not conscious of it at all. If someone hits us our usual response is to hit them back. What if we stop and ask: Why are they hitting me? What did I do to deserve this? The real answer could be that in a past life we hit them. The subconscious memory of events in past lives can give rise to the instinct to act. This is the instinctive astral at work. If we can raise ourselves up to our 'I-being' and pause to consider what is happening, this gives us the opportunity to think about the other person's position. This short circuits our instincts and instead of an "eye for eye" we become thoughtful, and can consider a more appropriate response.

The kinds of things we might think of can vary according to the situation, not everything is about our own karma, we could just be an actor on the stage of another person's karma. If we steal from someone it could be that they stole something from us in a past life. If we are stolen from, the other person may be taking back from us what they think is rightfully theirs. It may not necessarily be a physical possession that is taken; it could have been a place in the temple that was stolen.

Karma particularly plays out in our emotions. Anger can be the result of some injustice done in a past life. Love for others could be because we were unloved in another life. If we observe carefully, the pattern becomes clear and we always have the opportunity to restore the balance.

Another way karma emerges is through our likes and dislikes. If we really think about it, many of the things we like and dislike have no cause in the life we are living now despite what psychologists may say. How could we possibly explain not liking someone we just met? To understand this we need to look at the activity of our soul. In the book "I Connecting" I wrote

"Our 'I' is our inner strength.

There are many ways to identify the I-connection. For instance, we may feel our 'I' standing in our being like the mast of a tall ship. We can also experience it as calm and peace as we try to raise our emotions to a higher level. For example, if we feel animosity for someone, we can try to lighten that feeling and make it less intense. If we can't eliminate it but can move to a milder dislike, or to a feeling of mild annoyance, then our 'I' is connecting and assisting us to be more objective. Another approach is to find one thing to like about the person. It is when we do things like this that we can become more aware of the experience of our 'I' in our soul. This will add strength to thinking. It will also assist us to create new habits, think about things in new ways, and then our 'I' will be in charge of our soul more often. This will also prevent the soul from excluding the 'I' which it is often inclined to do." Kristina Kaine

The purpose of our karma is to assist us to become aware of our 'I', the more we resist this, the harder our karma will be. Deep within, every human being is driven to know their 'I', and until we do we experience deep dissatisfaction. We usually deal with this dissatisfaction by seeking to satisfy ourselves in many unhelpful ways. We can drink too much, take drugs, or dominate other people, gamble and much more. It is helpful to know that at the heart of it is the drive to experience our 'I'. If we can get a taste of our 'I' we will then become addicted to it and all other addictions will fall away.

All this can leave us asking why is the human 'I' so elusive. We find the answer when we understand that human beings have an evolving consciousness. According to Rudolf Steiner we developed the ability to have personal feelings during the period from 3000BC to 747BC. Then we began to develop the ability to think for ourselves which took us up to 1413AD at which time we began to work with our will and this is where we are at currently. We received our 'I-being' while we worked on our ability to think but we were not aware of it until we began developing our will. We will not be fully able to use our will consciously until 3573AD, so we have a way to go but that is no reason for not working with it now.

The thing about our will is that it gives us a sense of freedom which gives rise to the idea that 'I can do anything'. In fact, the will combined with the 'I' is very powerful indeed. This is our challenge, to be aware of the will and its inclination to be instinctive, and to raise it up to its highest conscious expression through our 'I'. One of the best ways to become conscious of the will is through the backwards exercise. Rudolf Steiner describes it in this way:

An exercise which is particularly valuable is at evening to allow the

experience of the day to pass in part vividly before the soul, beginning with the last event of evening and progressing toward the morning. Everything must be taken as atomistically [in minute detail] as possible; one must go so far as to imagine the ascent of a staircase in reverse, as if it were a descent from the top to the lowest step. The more one forms ideas in this way in an unaccustomed sequence which is not dependent on the external facts, the more one liberates the will, which is accustomed to abandon itself passively to the external facts, from these, and also from the physical body. From "Reincarnation and Immortality" October 9, 1916

Awakening to the will in our soul and body is a very valuable tool to assist us to connect with our 'I' and let go of our instinctive egotistical tendencies. When our 'I' is more active in our soul we become much more objective. We can look at our past passively and perhaps be grateful for the experiences that have brought us to this moment in time.

After doing such exercises, further support can be won through others which I would like to call "exercises in serious self contemplation and self education." One must be able to judge one's own actions and impulses of will with the same objective detachment as one can judge the actions and impulses of will of another personality. One must become in a sense the objective observer of one's own resolves and actions. From "Reincarnation and Immortality" October 9, 1916

Another reason for strengthening our will is because as we connect more frequently with our 'I' we begin to see our motives more clearly. This can bring up feelings of shame and regret - these feelings are not helpful. I often say that with the 'I' we can be the interested observer. I say 'interested' because we have to bring up some warmth of feeling otherwise we can be too cold and hard, which disconnects us from reality.

The main purpose of all of this is to learn to see that the way we act in this life has its cause in a past life. Of course we can show that our upbringing and our circumstances in life led us to behave in a certain way, but the root cause is always in a past life. Our upbringing and circumstances simply facilitate our destiny and karma.

Further to this, Rudolf Steiner says,

"What I prepare in this life will have its rewards in another."
February 9, 1906

This means that we have this opportunity to prepare until
the day we die. One wrong step does not cancel our
opportunity to make the right step. Our karma can be so
strong in certain areas that we are continually drawn to the
urge to retaliate, yet we must also continually try to meet this
urge with understanding and compassion (for ourselves first)
if we are to free ourselves from the consequences of our
actions in past lives. Yet often we don't, we are so blinded by
the karma we unconsciously do the opposite of what is
needed to create balance.

When it is all said and done, we must realize that:

*"In reality, karma is a redemption of man by himself, by dint of his
own efforts as he gradually ascends to freedom through the series of
incarnations."* An Esoteric Cosmology, Lecture 17 Redemption
and Liberation by Rudolf Steiner

Having the Mind of Christ

*"So if there is any encouragement in Christ, any incentive of love, any
participation in the Spirit, any affection and sympathy, complete my joy
by being of the same mind, having the same love, being in full accord and
of one mind. Do nothing from selfishness or conceit, but in humility count
others better than yourselves. Let each of you look not only to his own
interests, but also to the interests of others. Have this mind among
yourselves, which is yours in Christ Jesus, who, though he was in the
form of God, did not count equality with God a thing to be grasped, but
emptied himself, taking the form of a servant, being born in the likeness
of men. And being found in human form he humbled himself and
became obedient unto death, even death on a cross. Therefore God has
highly exalted him and bestowed on him the name which is above every
name, that at the name of Jesus every knee should bow, in heaven and on
earth and under the earth, and every tongue confess that Jesus Christ is*

Lord, to the glory of God the Father." Philippians 2:1-11

"Have this mind", St Paul says, the same mind that was in the Initiate Jesus. From this exalted position, to which every knee should bow, be a servant, be humble and be obedient.

It would be good to explore three simple words. They are very common words, they are used every day be everybody in all walks of life. The real meaning of these words is misunderstood. To truly understand these words means that we will develop the right relationship with our I AM and with the etheric Christ in our midst.

These three simple words are love, freedom and contentment.

Paul says that to have the mind of Christ all we need to do is serve and through our own determination to do it with love, freedom, and contentment and leave the rest to God.

What a simple message: serve with love, freedom and contentment.

They are human experiences which everyone in the civilized world expects to have, strives to have ... and rushes off for counselling when they don't have them!

The real meaning of these three experiences escapes 99% of the population. These simple human experiences: love, freedom, and contentment are actually abilities, forces that must develop within us, not things we must have. They are abilities that are full of mystery, full of potential because they create powers that release us from a purely material perception and give us the mind of Christ.

The world today interprets them so very materialistically.

o   Love often means finding Mr or Miss Right, or liking a thing rather than disliking it;

o   Freedom usually means not having any responsibilities or being on holiday; and o   Contentment means being happy, eating a good meal, having a few drinks, or going on a spending spree.

It is hard to believe that we can have the mind of Christ through these things! Of course it is a ridiculous notion. So what are these three things really? Well,

o   Contentment is Wonder,

o   Freedom is Conscience, and

o   Love is Compassion.

Wonder, Conscience and Compassion are tools for the growth and health of the soul and the I AM. As we develop them our consciousness grows and matures into the mind of Christ. The more highly developed our ability to experience Wonder, Conscience and Compassion is, the more we will express the third consciousness. And the more we will be released from the limitations of the physical … and the more clairvoyant we will be.

What are these three tools?

Wonder is to marvel, to feel awe. To stop to smell the flowers. To acknowledge spirit moving within matter. This is true contentment, which harmonizes our feelings.

Conscience is about putting ourselves in the other person's shoes. Do unto others. It is also about listening to the voice within which says, "Don't do that, or do this." When we know that voice intimately we experience true freedom.

Compassion is to relinquish our personal position and experiencing things as if we were the other person. This is true love and it is integral to the process of forgiveness. Forgiving others for what they do to us, forgiving ourselves for what we do, forgiving others for not fully expressing their potential; and also forgiving ourselves for not expressing our own potential.

It is interesting that these three words did not exist two and half thousand years ago. Search the literature, you will not find them. Then as you search you will suddenly see them creeping in. Why is this? Well, mankind lived hand in hand with spirit and the spiritual beings who gave us these experiences externally. Then as spirit withdrew mankind had to develop their own inner ways to do what spirit had done from the outside. This is the work of the I AM.

When these experiences began happening within us we had to think up words to describe them. If you think deeply about these three words they have much to reveal. To discover their mysteries is to invoke their power. Let's have a closer look at them.

Wonder

Wonder is about stopping to smell the flowers but it is not only about that. The soul feels wonder when it sees something it can't explain. Something it hasn't seen before. It also experiences wonder when it sees something and has a feeling it's seen it before but it was different.

Think about seeing something you haven't seen before. Imagine what it would be like to see an airplane for the first time. That would we awesome. People experienced wonder when they saw the first car or first train. They thought there were horses inside the train propelling it along.

What about when something looks familiar but it isn't quite. Consider that everything your soul sees in the physical world it has seen from a different perspective before birth when you were in the spiritual world. What was it like before you incarnated to perceive the sun? You didn't have physical eyes. How does the memory of that affect you when you watch the rising or setting sun from the earth perspective?

Why is it that we don't often feel wonder at things we see in dreams which if we saw them when we are awake would fill us with wonder. Like when we fly in a dream we think it is a natural, normal thing to do. Compare that with how you would feel if you saw someone flying unaided through the air.

The more we can marvel, feel awe and wonder, the more we build the mind of Christ and increase our ability to see him. Wonder at nature, don't be indifferent, and don't be clinical. Appreciate human worth, the worth of yourself and worth of others. Wonder at it. The more wonder a soul can experience the more alive we are.

Jane Goodall, the English woman who studied the chimpanzees spoke of a mystical experience she had. It was after the death of her husband and she returned to the forest to the chimps: *"I was sitting in forest just feeling it when suddenly I heard the sound of it. Thousands of sounds that I had never heard before. I knew that I was hearing what the chimps heard."*

I am not sure what chimps hear but she experienced true wonder, she experienced spirit. She speaks to people all over the world about her experiences in the forest with the chimps and she touches them deeply, they often cry. To me that is Christ working - that fills me with wonder.

Wonder therefore happens when we transcend our physical self and recognize that which is not revealed through our senses. That is true contentment.

Conscience

Conscience – is a power that guides our actions. It is about putting ourselves in the other person's shoes. Perceiving what is right, and what is not right. It has to do with perception therefore the more finely tuned this ability the more clairvoyant we are.

We know only too well that earthly life is plagued by desires. We are driven to pursue the things that please us and we try to stay clear of things that don't please us. People talk about their demons as if they are beings that make them do things, want things, demand this or that of them. Ancient

Greek literature speaks of demons, they called them the Furies. If you did something wrong, you didn't have a pang of conscience within you but a demonic form, the Furies, appeared before you tormentingly.

When we transcend our impulses; our likes and dislikes, we experience the voice of correction. The voice of conscience and the power of it separates us from our desires. We can work with it by using our will. "To think twice" about something is the phrase that expresses this power of conscience.

When we don't listen to the voice of conscience we retaliate in an attempt to ward off the unpleasant situation. If we think twice and listen to our conscience we come to the "it doesn't matter" realization. To face a situation with an "it doesn't matter in the scheme of things" attitude is what conscience wants.

The power of conscience is relentless. If we ignore our conscience during the day it is difficult to get to sleep at night, we toss and turn. We cannot enter the purity of the spiritual worlds with a tormented conscience. This is one of the reasons it is good to go through our day backward at the end of day because we can evaluate the moments when our will did not balance out our desires.

It is helpful to think about the times the power of our conscience has compelled us to do a thing or not to do a thing. We can come to recognize this guiding power that is ours to use as we will – in freedom.

Compassion

Compassion, love, forgiveness are abilities that transcend our personal position. Then we can transcend our 'I' and pass over into the other person's 'I' and see things from their point of view or walk in their shoes.

Then we can feel their joy or pain, their success, their failure as if it were our own. Not abstractly but as our own.

Real tears rise up in us, real joy.

True compassion, true love, dissolves all differences. Compassion is the power by which we can see beyond outer impressions and really experience the other person. Compassion is not sentimental, it is not a feeling. It involves the mind, it is knowledge, real knowledge of the other person, we marry compassion and thinking.

Forgiveness is an integral part of compassion; forgiving others for what they do to us, forgiving ourselves for our short comings, forgiving others for not fully expressing their own potential and also forgiving ourselves for not expressing our own potential. Resist the inclination to be hard on self and on others.

Love and compassion are the hallmarks of my teacher, Rev Mario Schoenmaker's ministry. His great love for Christ and his great love for his people, a love which we must continue in our own way. Such a love is strong but gentle, and it is uncompromising. It is a love that could be nailed to a cross if that was the task. A love so great that a high spiritual being could incarnate into the body of a man.

It is good for us to contemplate the ways we love, the ways we show compassion, the ways we forgive. It is important to understand the role our mind plays in that.

These powers of Contentment, Freedom and Love or Wonder, Conscience and Compassion are our ticket into the spiritual spheres; they assist us to transcend our personal position, our physical earthly position. Through them we can forge a closer relationship with our I AM.

o In wonder we leave the world of the physical senses,

o in compassion we leave our own personal position,

o in conscience we leave our desires.

When we leave the sense world around us we enter into the spirit behind the physical; when we leave our 'I' we enter into the 'I' of the other person; when we leave our desires we enter into the Cosmos. This expansion of our being assists and strengthens the etheric presence of Christ. We cannot develop the right relationship with our I AM if Christ is not involved. The closer we get to engaging with our I AM, and the more we involve Christ in that process, the more we will be lights in the darkness. The spiritual worlds wait for this with eager longing.

The greatest tool we have with which to develop these powers or forces within us is our mind, our thinking. So hear St Paul say, "Have this mind among yourselves, which is yours in Christ Jesus".

When the mind of Christ is ours, the Christ becomes a mighty force in this world. One Christ who dissolves all differences. That is the true meaning of Love, Freedom and Contentment.

* * *

GLOSSARY OF TERMS

Including some Biblical Greek terms explained in English

Adultery: *moichos*, an adulterer metaphorically means one who is faithless toward God; they have lost sight of the God with whom they dwelt as spiritual beings. In other words, there has been a breach in the relationship between the soul and the spirit. The soul is more attracted to worldly things and is not interested to do the work necessary to achieve, of its own accord, the mastery required to individually and personally experience spiritual insight.

Ahriman: Called Satan, a force of opposition hindering our consciousness. This being is associated with qualities of calculating and coldness which bind us to materialistic outlooks.

Angel: *angelos* means messenger. Angels are intermediaries who help and guide the evolution of human consciousness. They carry messages to us from the spiritual worlds as well as from us to the beings who wisely guide the

Universe. They are one stage above human beings as animals are one stage below.

Ascension: The dissolving of the resurrection body. This takes place 40 days after Easter.

Astral body: The force of motion and emotion within us. Through it we are conscious beings.

Astral world: Just as we have an astral and etheric body, so too does this earth.

Awake: *gregoreo* means more than being awake; it means to be watchful, to be vigilant.

Behold: *idou* is one of twelve different Greek words for behold and it points to seeing beneath the surface of things to the spiritual reality.

Blessed: *makarios* from the root *mak* meaning large, long, or expanded. Today we might say macro, big.

Blood: The physical expression of our I - it is the fire within us.

Body, Soul and Spirit: *soma, psuche* and *pneuma.*

Soma is body as a whole, our physical expression which includes the vehicle to express our actions which is associated with our will.

Psuche is soul, from which we have the word psychology. *Psuche* can be translated in the Bible as heart, life, mind, or soul. In our soul our feelings are dominant.

Pneuma can be translated as breath, life, spirit, or wind. Thinking is the dominant activity.

This text from 1 Thessalonians mentions spirit, soul and body .

May the God of peace himself sanctify you wholly; and may your spirit (*pneuma*) and soul (*psuche*) and body (*soma*) be kept sound and blameless at the coming of our Lord Jesus Christ. 1 Thessolonians 5:23

Christ: The Cosmic Being who entered into the body of Jesus.

Clairvoyance: occurs when the connection between the astral and the etheric is loosened so that the astral can stamp spiritual truth into the etheric.

Conquering: *nikao* really means overcoming; to 'come over' from the past into the present.

Compassion: does not mean experiencing the other one's pain, it means experiencing the other person's value as a human being. Compassion arises out of the purest love and respect for the other person. We see the other person as a divine being.

Conscience: is an inner voice judging our actions and thoughts. We could say that it is an organ of cognition revealing to us what is right and wrong; this means that it is up to us to develop a good conscience. The more highly developed our conscience the closer we come to Christ.

Consciousness Soul: is strengthened when we use our will and act in the world. The purpose of the consciousness soul is to develop independence, self-reliance. We must purify our Consciousness Soul in such a way that the Spirit Self can arise within it.

Ego: Ich German. I or self – that which says I to itself. The fourth member of mankind.

Etheric Body: The life-force which is a web of formative forces giving our physical body shape.

Etheric of the Earth: It is like an airy water filled garment from which all things receive their life.

Etheric Presence of Christ: The crucified Christ Jesus cast off his physical body and reappeared in his life-body or etheric presence.

Esoteric: Means just beneath the surface.

Esoteric Christians: Non-denominational 'generic' Christians who study the inner meaning of the teachings of Christ.

Evil: Forces of opposition. The forces of progress gained strength by resistance to opposition.

Faith: *pistis*, means 'firm persuasion, a conviction based on hearing'. When we have faith we know something with certainty. Faith is a cognitive experience not a substitute for cognition.

Father: The stillness, the primal spirit. The spiritual substance that weaves and lives through the world as spirit.

Flesh: *sarx* means desire and indicates our astral body.

Follow: *akoloutheo* literally means alike-way and gives the sense of becoming like Jesus, copying the way he is.

Forgive: *aphiemi*, means to send from.

Freedom: Equals spiritual activity; physical activity is not freedom. Freedom is not created by the gods but it is a process arising out of man. Freedom can only be experienced in the soul.

Glory: *doxa* from dokeo, to seem, and often points to the faculty of Imagination

Golgotha: This event saved our soul from dying.

Grace: *charis* is the generation of abundance out of nothing. The ability to have full control over all our feelings, thoughts and actions.

Heaven: *ouranos* means to rise or lift – to heave. An indication of the effort needed to raise our consciousness to a higher level.

Holy Spirit: *parakletos* para means beside, and *kaleo* means to call. To call to one's side, translated as the comforter which comforts us so that we can bear what we see.

I Am: *ego eimi*, the Higher Self or True Self.

Imagination, Inspiration and Intuition: These are the eyes of the spirit. They are three stages of knowledge. Through them we live into the higher world.

Imagination: The ability to perceive behind the sense world and see the outer form of spirit.

Initiation: Achieving a higher consciousness through personal effort.

Inspiration: The ability to communicate with the beings of the soul and spirit world. To hear the inner world.

Intellectual Soul: Or mind soul, rational soul, developed 800BC - 1400AD

Intuition: Merging or entering into other beings so that they are known from within them.

Jehovah: One of the seven Elohim, leaders on old moon who progressed far enough to pour forth love. While man was still unable to see the outer world Jehovah instilled ego-consciousness into him.

Jesus: Represents the human being purified by connecting fully with the I Am.

Judgment: *krisis* means a separating, then a decision, which can take time. *Krisis* is associated with the critical thinking required for making the right decision.

Karma: The redemption of man by himself.

Life: *bios* is physical life associated with the body. *psuche* is soul life associated with emotions. *zoe*, spiritual life associated with consciousness and thought.

Logos: It not only means word but also, and more generally, ratio or relationship – living connections that, binding together and holding apart, create a coherent whole identity.

Lord: *kyrios* – I AM, the ruler of the soul forces.

Love: There are four different Greek words for love.

Eros - Erotic physical love. This is passionate love, with sensual desire and longing. Through this love the procreative urge arises for survival of the species.

Philia - Brotherly and sisterly love which can be supportive and nurturing but can also be exclusive. It is usually a gentle, understanding, and life-giving love that is found in true friendship.

Storge - Love of family, tribe, and nation. It can be defensive and aggressive to those outside the group. This is the kind of love we also find in the animal kingdom.

Agape - Divine love, Christ-filled love. This is the love expressed by those who experience the highest in themselves, which they express without fear or favor. It speaks of unification and intense compassion. It may not always be interpreted as love because in its expression it can cut like a sword. "I come with a sword" *Matthew* 10:34

Lucifer: Called the Devil, associated with qualities of warmth and enthusiasm. This being tempts us with shortcuts and encourages us to be lazy.

Matter: Matter is shattered spiritual form.

Meek: *praus* could suggest weakness, but it is actually the opposite. It takes the strongest person to maintain an inner gentleness when dealing with difficulty.

Mercy: *eleemones*, really means that we feel the same as the other person. We are at one with them, we are so harmonized with them that we share their experiences as if we were them.

Morality: We are moral beings when we don't acquire our happiness at the expense of others. Morality is pure, sense-free will. The root of morality is love. To be a moral person has consequences beyond our physical life as Rudolf Steiner explains, "Our good deeds originate in our interest in other people. At death, the etheric body of a person who lived morally retains its human shape. These forces participate in the reshaping of the cosmos." Earthly Knowledge and Heavenly Wisdom by Rudolf Steiner

Occult: Hidden. Occult is the highest wisdom which only appears when we bring our own light to meet it.

Peace: *eirene* indicates freedom from disturbance, stillness. We experience peace when we achieve inner harmony, when we are not disturbed. *Shalom* is the Hebrew equivalent and means soundness. Three times Jesus says, "*Eirene humin*", "Peace to you" which essentially means remove the disturbance within you and reinstate soundness.

Pentecost: Whitsun, the Holy Spirit descends on mankind, the gift of the Father is given so that we become self-conscious beings.

Poor: *ptochos* from *ptosso* to crouch. It speaks of a contraction.

Power: *exousia* in Greek, in Hebrew it is *Elohim*, the word used in Genesis translated as God. It means the power to create.

Prayer: *proseuchomai,* is not egotistical begging, prayer is a willingness to be led beyond ourselves towards the truth.

Prophet: *prophetes* means to speak before; *pro* means before plus the root of *phanai* which means 'to speak'. Prophets are those who can speak about things before they happen so that we recognize them when they do happen. This helps us to recognize something new when it arises.

Pure: *katharos* which suggests catharsis, purging, purifying and cleansing. The purifying process we undertake is cathartic, especially when we purify our emotions.

Reincarnation: Each human being lives repeated earthly lives in either a male or female body.

Resurrection: On one hand, the attaining of a higher consciousness even while on Earth, in the physical body, and, on the other hand, the complete preservation of individual ego-consciousness in the ascent into the higher worlds after death.

Repent: *metanoeo*, literally means to perceive afterwards. It implies that we can see the results of our actions before we act. This assists us to change the way we act, think, and feel because we see the aftereffects. To see 'in real time' the affect we have on the future changes everything about us.

Righteousness: *dikaiosune*, means justice in terms of being just, balanced and in harmony. Justice is a continual series of adjustments to restore balance and harmony.

Sacrifice: Giving, no longer taking.

Saints: *hagios*, are those who have entered into a holy love for the mysteries. Gentiles, ethnos, really means the people generally as opposed the select few.

See: *idou* means see, it means seeing the hidden detail because it is able to engage the purified faculties of thinking, feeling and will.

Sentient Soul: Produces living sensations. Expresses how the soul is adjusted to life, harmoniously or not.

Sin: *hamartia*, means missing the mark, it means that we haven't achieved our goal; we need to improve our aim.

Son of God: Human from birth to development of the I consciousness

Son of man: Human who has developed I consciousness.

Soul: *psuche,* the place in our being where the forces of feeling, thinking, and will are active.

Spirit: *pneuma,* the third region of the human being, above the soul, or finer than the soul, where Imagination, Inspiration and Intuition are active. The Spirit is in perpetual action; it forms the various parts of matter, matter follows the moving spirit.

Thinking: The elements of thinking appeared only during the last ages of the Atlantean epoch.

Truth: *alethes,* not forgotten or remembering what we have forgotten - unforgetting.

Living water: *hydor zao,* refers to the element of water rather than the fluidic substance itself. The element of water is the etheric. In its highest form, the Life Ether, it is the expression of Christ. When our etheric life force is transformed and organized by the I Am it is ready to receive the Christ Spirit.

White: *leukos* and comes from *luke* meaning light or light-filled.

Will: The directive forces. Will at work in the body is unconscious / untransparent. We strengthen the will through meditation and backwards exercise so that it comes conscious in soul and spirit.

Wisdom: Using what was won in past incarnations in the present incarnation. Wisdom leads a man through self to selflessness.

Witness: *marturia* doesn't mean to witness something at a distance but rather to enter into a living experience, as if it was happening in the moment to us.

ABOUT THE AUTHOR

Kristina Kaine has worked with people all her life: during her early career in medical sales and staff recruitment, and since 1987 in her own business which matches people in business partnerships. Through this rich interaction with people, Kristina has observed the struggle for self identity from many angles.

She was awakened to the ideas of Rudolf Steiner by Rev Mario Schoenmaker, attending all of Schoenmaker's lectures for 14 years. After Schoenmaker's death in 1997, Kristina realised the need to explain the knowledge of the threefold human being in simple terms that could be applied easily in daily life. She has set this out in her book, 'I Connecting : the Soul's Quest', which was published in 2007 by Robert Sardello through Goldenstone Press. It is not unusual for Kristina to receive comments about her book like this: "It seems like a very lucid treatment, like looking through a clear glass window through which one can discover and recognize the landscape of the soul."

Since 2003 Kristina has written weekly reflections which apply this knowledge of the threefold human being to Bible texts. This is not done in the context of any particular religious beliefs but from a broader perspective that all religions could apply. These reflections are distributed by email and are read worldwide. They are available as Kindle ebooks and paperback through Amazon.

Kristina is also a blogger, on Face Book, on her own sites and on Huffington Post.

RESOURCES

Websites

Visit Kristina's Website http://esotericconnection.com

Buy Kristina's books on Amazon

http://www.amazon.com/Kristina-Kaine/e/B00AEW92B2

Join Kristina's fans on Face Book

https://www.facebook.com/EsotericConnection

Research Material used

Access many of Rudolf Steiner's lectures on this website https://www.rsarchive.org/

The Bible, Revised Standard Version

Expository Dictionary of New Testament Words : W. E. Vine

Greek and Hebrew translations: https://www.studylight.org/

Other books as quoted throughout.

Books by Kristina Kaine

Available on Amazon https://www.amazon.com/Kristina-Kaine/e/B00AEW92B2/

Most of Kristina's books were written as weekly Reflections or blog posts, as follows.

1. I AM Sayings : January 2003 – September 2003
2. Christian Initiation : September 2003 – May 2004
3. Eightfold Path : June 2004 – December 2004
4. Twelve Disciples : 2005
5. Seven Signs : January - July 2006
6. Beatitudes in St John's Gospel: August 2006 – March 2007
7. The Revelation to John : April 2007 – April 2010
8. Who is Jesus : What is Christ : May 2010 – 2016 5 volumes
9. The Holy Nights 2011 - 2016
10. To Journey Back: October 2016 4 Volumes so far by 2019
11. I Connecting : The Soul's Quest published in July 2007
12. I Connecting Work Book
13. I Connecting Exercises
14. Bible Unlocked 2009 - 2019
15. Contemplating the Christian Festivals 2003 - expect to publish 2019

Made in the USA
Columbia, SC
09 July 2020